GRASPING
THE
GRAPE

GRASPING THE GRAPE

Demystifying grape
varieties to help you
discover the wines
you love

MARYSE CHEVRIERE

Illustrated by Sarah Tanat-Jones

Hardie Grant

BOOKS

More than anything,
this one's for you, Mom and Dad.

Contents

Introduction

When people ask me how I got into wine, my answer is always the same: 'Very, *very* reluctantly'.

It's not that I didn't love wine, or that I found it boring, or that I thought of it as just another alcoholic drink; quite the opposite. The problem is it's almost too interesting, too complex, too broad. Why, it's even got its own unique language. And then there's the science-y component, the geographical knowledge required, and the fact that it's subjective and constantly evolving. I mean, someone pour me a glass of wine so I can process all this stuff that I have to learn about wine! To cut a long story short, I started out feeling like you probably do about the subject: completely overwhelmed and totally unsure of where to begin.

For me, the easiest, most logical starting point was grapes, and so that is the focus of this book. The following pages will outline the world's major red and white varietals and give you a snapshot of what you need to know about them to embark on a more informed wine-drinking journey. Basics like notable growing regions and food pairings are covered with each, as well as more practical things for consumers such as general tasting descriptors to help you convey what you like or don't (the 'Key Words') and examples of other grapes you might like.

Supporting this core information are nuggets of the most useful, practical tips you might need: the 'dos and don'ts' of storing and serving, FAQs about rosé, how to understand key wine descriptors through side-by-side tastings, a cheat sheet on deciphering labels, a whirlwind tour of the world of sparkling wine and a glossary of technical and sommelier terms.

Don't see this as your complete guide to everything wine-related but, rather, your friendly (pocket-sized!) overview of the essentials. So, please, drink up, and remember to have fun and keep learning.

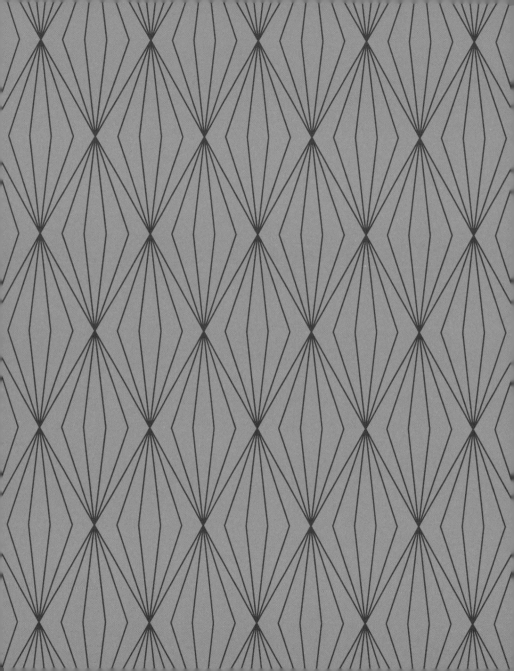

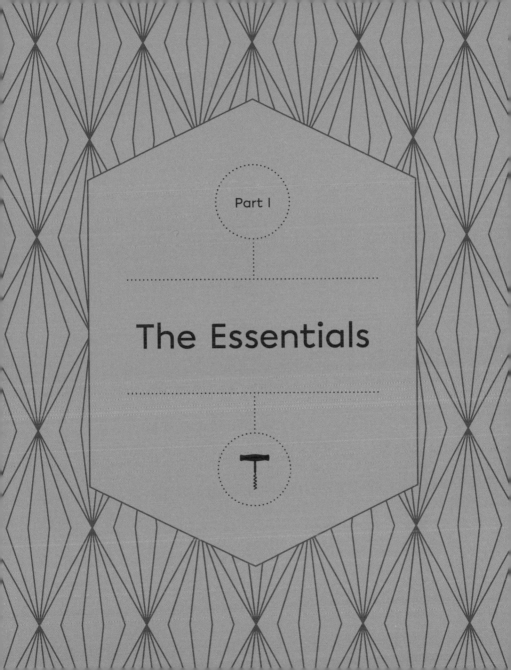

Part I

The Essentials

Anatomy of a Wine Label: The Essentials

Front

Producer Name

Often the easiest item to pick out on a label as it tends to be the most prominent, this is the name of who made the wine. In France, look for the prefix *'Domaine'* or *'Château'*; in Germany and Austria, *'Weingut'*; in Italy, *'Castello'*, *'Cantina'* or *'Tenuta'*; *'Quinta'* in Portuguese and, in Spanish-speaking countries, *'Bodegas'*. Sometimes also a wine may go by a branded name that is a subsidiary of a large-scale producer (most often you'll see this with a New World wine, the US especially).

Vintage

The year the grapes were harvested.

Region/Appellation/Sub-Appellation/Vineyard Name

When it comes to wines from the EU, the broad strokes perspective is that the more specific the growing site listed, the higher quality the wine is going to be. It's like a hospital consultant with a lot of letters after their name: it means they've had to pass more tests and meet more standards, and are therefore more unique and prized because of it.

Regional Classification

For example, *Appellation d'Origine Contrôlée* (AOC) in France; *Indicazione Geografica Tipica* (IGT), *Denominazione di Origine Controllata* (DOC) and *Denominazione di Origine Controllata e Garantita* (DOCG) in Italy; *Denominación de Origen* (DO/DOC) in Spain; *Districtus Austriae Controllatus* (DAC) in Austria; *Denominação de Origem Controlada* (DOC) in Portugal and *American Viticultural Area* (AVA) in the US. These regulatory bodies determine the rules and regulations for the region's growing practices and standards.

Vineyard Site Quality Level Indicator

In France, look for words like *'Premier Cru'* and the even more prized *'Grand Cru'*; in Germany, keep an eye out for either *'VDP Grosse Lage'* or *'VDP Grosses Gewachs'*, but you should also expect to pay a lot more for these wines. Just remember: not all regions – even some of the top

ones, like Barolo – have a built-in quality classification hierarchy for their vineyard sites, so be careful not to look for one as an absolute, across-the-board prerequisite.

Aging Indicator
In the EU, the word 'Reserve' (aka *Riserva/Reserva/Gran Reserva*) indicates that the wine has been aged for a period of time prior to release. The amount of time depends on the region's particular regulated standards. Again, expect these to be more expensive. Important side note though: the term is not protected in New World regions like the U.S. and Australia.

Sweetness Level Indicator
Most commonly seen on bottles of German Riesling, which can range from dry *(Trocken)* to off-dry *(Kabinett)* to sweet *(Spätlese)* to very sweet *(Auslese)* (just an FYI: Technically, those last three terms refer to the ripeness level of the grapes at harvest time, but by and large it will coordinate with the sweetness level of the wine). These will appear as a suffix to the grape varietal. Another good example would be on labels of Chenin Blanc from Vouvray, which will tell you the wine is off-dry with the words *'Demi-sec'* or sweet with the word *'Moelleux'*.

Grape Varietal
This is more common practice with New World wines and wines from Austria and Germany, although it is becoming more prevalent throughout Old World regions. This is the grape that makes up the overwhelming majority, if not 100%, of the wine.

Bottle Size
Measured in millilitres, the standard bottle size is 750 ml (25.4 fl oz). Half bottles come in 375 ml (12.7 fl oz) bottles, while magnums are double the standard size at 1.5 l (50.8 fl oz).

ABV
Literally, the Alcohol by Volume. Most dry red and white wines fall in the 12–13.5% range. Lower than 12% in a white and you can expect it to be a little sweet, and reds clocking in at over 14% are likely to be full, rich and boozy.

Back

Importer and/or Distributor
The company responsible for sourcing and shipping the wine from its country of origin and distributing it for sale in its current location. Essentially, the wine's talent agent.

Government Warning
Most countries include a government-mandated warning, either via symbol or text, indicating that consuming alcohol impairs your ability to drive, is not advised for pregnant women, and may be detrimental to your health.

Product of [Country Name]

Estate Bottled
As straightforward as it sounds, this means the wine was bottled by the producer at the winery where it was made. For French wines, you might alternatively see *'mis en bouteille au domaine/à la propriété'*.

Contains Sulphites
Sulphites are a natural by-product of the winemaking process and are not to be blamed for your hangover. All wines contain sulphites, hence the listing on the label, but not all wines have added sulphites. If you're concerned about your wine having extra sulphites in it – it's a commonly used preservative agent – look for wines labeled with 'no added sulphites' ('natural' wines are a good place to start this quest).

Label Decoder:
The Grapes Behind the
Regional Place Names

Wine labels offer a lot of information. Some of it is easy and straightforward to understand; for example, a wine's alcohol content and vintage, or who imports it into the country. Other key details, like, say, what grape(s) the wine is made up of, are not always as obvious. It's not so of much an issue with New World wines (aka North America, South Africa and Southern Hemisphere countries such as Australia, New Zealand and Argentina), which generally require listing the primary or single varietal on the label. Less user-friendly, however, are those wines from Old World regions – particularly France and Italy – which use important place names on the label as a kind of pseudonym for the varietal.

It's not intended to be misleading by design; really, it's about celebrating the terroir (your catch-all term for 'sense of place', see page 161) and the fact that certain grapes have been found to grow best in certain locations. Still, for the not-quite-yet-in-the-know, the system can definitely act as a barrier. It facilitates common, rookie-mistake claims such as, 'I won't drink Sauvignon Blanc – hate the stuff – but I like pretty much everything else. I've been enjoying Sancerre a lot lately.' Here's the thing, the white wines produced in sancerre can only be made from 100% Sauvignon Blanc. But – and this is important – if you've ever made this statement before, please don't feel embarrassed, as it's still a really useful indication of your tastes to the sommelier or wine professional helping you make a selection. All it means is that you like a specific style of Sauvignon Blanc.

However, if you want to avoid any such slip-ups, the following is a cheat sheet for some of the most common place names found on labels and their associated grape varietals.

Whites

Chablis = 100% Chardonnay
Pouilly-Fuissé = 100% Chardonnay
Sancerre = 100% Sauvignon Blanc
(the exception being if it's a red or rosé,
it's made from Pinot Noir)
Pouilly Fumé = 100% Sauvignon Blanc
Vouvray = 100% Chenin Blanc
Savennières = 100% Chenin Blanc
Muscadet = 100% Melon de Bourgogne
Condrieu = 100% Viognier
Tokaji = Mostly Furmint, as well as
Hárslevelű and Muscat Blanc
Sauternes = Mostly Sémillon, with some
percentage of Sauvignon Blanc and
Muscadelle
Soave = Mostly Garganega, with up to
30% Trebbiano
Vinho Verde = Mostly Loureiro and
Alvarinho
Gavi = 100% Cortese
White Burgundy = Chardonnay

Reds

Beaujolais = 100% Gamay
Barolo = 100% Nebbiolo
Barbaresco = 100% Nebbiolo
Dogliani = 100% Dolcetto
Valtellina = Mostly Nebbiolo
Gattinara = Mostly Nebbiolo
Ghemme – Mostly Nebbiolo
Roero = Mostly Nebbiolo
Chianti = Mostly if not 100% Sangiovese
Brunello di Montalcino = 100% Sangiovese
Rosso di Montalcino = 100% Sangiovese
Vino Nobile di Montepulciano = Mostly
Sangiovese
Chinon = Mostly 100% Cabernet Franc
Bourgueil and
Saint-Nicolas-de-Bourgueil = Mostly
100% Cabernet Franc
Cornas = 100% Syrah
Hermitage = Mostly 100% Syrah
Crozes-Hermitage – Mostly 100% Syrah
Saint-Joseph = Mostly 100% Syrah
Gigondas = Mostly Grenache
Vacqueyras = Mostly Grenache
Chateâuneuf-du-Pape = Mostly Grenache,
Syrah, Mourvèdre and Cinsault, but
Clairette, Bourboulenc, Roussanne,
Vaccarèse, Counoise, Muscardin, Picpoul,
Picardan and Terret Noir are also permitted
Cahors = Mostly Malbec
Rioja = Mostly Tempranillo
Bandol = At least 50% Mourvèdre
Priorat = Mostly Grenache
Valpolicella and
Amarone della Valpolicella = Mostly
Corvina with Rondinella and Molinara
'Left Bank' Bordeaux red = Mostly
Cabernet Sauvignon
'Right Bank' Bordeaux red = Mostly Merlot
Red Burgundy = Pinot Noir

Become a Better Wine Shopper: Ten Tips

1. Seek out a good local wine shop

If you're interested in wine as more than just alcohol to put in a glass at the end of a long day, then this is essential. Sure, there are plenty of supermarkets out there with above-average wine selections, but a good wine shop offers important perks. For example, well-educated staff that are excited to engage with you and share their knowledge (sans condescension, pretension or any of that other nonsense that makes people feel intimidated about wine). Better yet, they will most likely offer to track your purchases and get to know your palate profile in order to make better recommendations in the future.

Often wine shops host tastings or classes for free or, if not, relatively inexpensively, where a winemaker or sales rep from an importer or distributor is pouring. Take advantage of this insider access; listen, drink and ask questions. Another valuable bonus of finding a good shop? Case (or half case) discounts. Learning about wine is not a cheap activity. Fortunately, most places offer deals when you purchase in larger quantities, such as six or 12 or more bottles, which means you get to save the cost of a bottle or two by committing to trying several.

2. Become a regular at a wine bar or restaurant with an extensive list of wines by the glass

A similar idea to the above. Find a place that has an interesting, unique selection and knowledgeable staff, but with one additional bonus: you can ask to try before you buy. Think of it as akin to being at an ice cream shop and getting to sample a couple flavours before making your decision – just don't be that person who tries six different types and then leaves, full, without buying a single scoop.

The kind of by-the-glass list we're talking about here probably has upwards of six different selections for red and white wines, multiple sparklings, (ideally) a couple of rosés as well, and most probably one or two apéritifs (sherries, vermouths) and dessert wines. The selection should rotate with some relative frequency, and include some things you are not that familiar with. Treat this as your classroom. Ask about the grape(s) and the producer, where the wine is from and what's special and characteristic of the style if it's something unusual. Ask to do half-glass pours so that you get to try a wider variety. If you find something you like, see if they know where you can buy it, and what other similar wines might be worth trying. Be curious, and don't be afraid to say you don't like something – again, it will help staff inform your choice next time around.

3. Take pictures of the labels of wines you like (and don't)

Because wine is a complicated language, and trying to explain what you're looking for can be a kind of, 'how do you know what you call "green" is the same as what I call "green"?' situation, pictures are helpful. And objective. Whether you track your hits and misses with the help of an app (Delectable and Vivino are two of the big ones) or simply keep a folder on your phone, a label shot is a good starting point for a conversation. Or, at the very least, it gives you a reference when you're scanning the shelves.

4. If you're not good with tasting notes, use context clues to help describe what you're looking for

Maybe you're still unsure of how to answer when asked if you're looking for something light or full-bodied; super dry or slightly juicy; fuller and rounder or lean and mineral-driven. Not to worry. If you're a little uncomfortable with tasting descriptors, offer some context clues to work with. How much you want to spend (and please, don't be shy about this), what food – if any – you're pairing it with, who you're drinking with and what the environment is going to be like are all useful pieces of information that can help inform a better selection. So think: is the bottle for you or just something to bring to a party? Or is it a gift? And if so, what's the occasion? Do you need something to go with the takeaway food you're about to pick up, or do you just want a bottle to go with cheese and charcuterie? Are you looking to splurge or keep it in a more wallet-friendly price range? Just don't shut down and say, 'oh I don't know, I just want a 'nice' wine.' What does that mean? Is the wine polite? Does it send you a card every year on your birthday? Chances are, if 'nice' is the only criteria you request, you aren't going to end up with anything special, or specifically to your taste or suitable for the occasion, as it's too generic.

5. Pay attention to who imports the wines you like

The front label is usually the first place we look to gather information about a wine. But what if it isn't enough? Even if you recognise the region or the grape and understand what that might translate to in the glass, the particular producer and their style can still be foreign to you. It's at this point in the game that you should turn over the bottle to look for your next clue: who imports the wine.

A key and powerful cog in the supply chain, the importer essentially functions as an agent. They seek out the talent that best represents their brand (for example, a particular winemaking philosophy or growing region) and then take on the responsibility of bringing it into the country and supporting its success. Recognising which importers represent your favourite wines is like identifying the people in the room who share your taste in music. While not a 100%-satisfaction-guaranteed tactic, it can at least offer a sense of reassurance and help encourage exploration beyond your old trusted standbys. And don't forget to use importers as a resource when you're checking out a new wine shop: if you see a lot of familiar names that you like, you're probably in the right place.

6. Look for the second-label wines and négociant projects of big-name producers

The basic premise is simple: big name, high-price-fetching estates only wants to use the best fruit from the best vineyards for their top bottlings. Unfortunately, that means a lot of very-good-just-not-quite-as-great fruit is left sitting there on the bench like some untapped resource. Instead of wasting it and taking a loss, the producer gives it a home under a different, more value-friendly second label.

Generally speaking, the concept is a win-win for both the estate and the consumer. The winery gets to maximise the use of their product yield while simultaneously opening themselves up to a market of consumers that might otherwise be priced out of their offerings. And you? Well, you get the B-team. A B-team that, yeah, may be younger and less experienced, but was still trained and raised around the A-team, and was even overseen by the same coaches and managers, the bonus being it's also a lot less expensive. The only tricky part, of course, is that often the names of these second-label projects are completely different and don't include any mention of the famous winery or winemaker that you might be familiar with. Occasionally the label will read [Second Label Name] with the words 'by [First Label Name]' somewhere in smaller print in the corner, so be sure to look out for that. Otherwise, you're going to need to do a little research and/or press the staff at your local shop for information.

7. Don't be too quick to judge screw-top wines

While the sentimental attachment to cork is understandable – after all, it's been the wine bottle closure of choice since the 15th century – we need to get over this ingrained prejudice towards its alternatives.

Just because a wine is bottled with a screw-top closure, it doesn't automatically mean it's cheap and poorly made. Sure, there's reason to be cautious; screw tops are a popular choice with lower-quality, mass-production wineries because of cost-efficiency, consumer convenience and the fact that they eliminate the possibility of wine becoming 'corked'. But it's not bad logic, actually, and therefore there's no reason why you should discriminate against screw-topped wine if you like and trust the producer or, at the very least, the shop selling the wine. In countries such as Austria, Australia and New Zealand, screw tops are pretty much the standard across the board.

8. Separate the genuinely useful and informative from the propaganda when it comes to shelf recommendations

If you're going to consult shelf recommendations (aka those little write-ups describing the bottle you're scoping out), be wary of the red flags. For example, a description that only talks about the wine's point scores. You could argue that a wine's 'point score' really says more about the winery's marketing budget than what's actually going on inside the bottle. So it got a 90-something rating. Great. Years in school have conditioned us to get excited about that kind of number but, when it comes to wine scores, what do you really even know about the marker or their scoring system anyway? Better to look for recommendations that read as personal and unique – bonus points if it's handwritten or if it has a staff member's name attached.

9. Looking for a dry white? Check the ABV

If you only remember one thing about the science of wine let it be this: yeast + sugar = alcohol + CO2. That, friends, is the basic formula for the fermentation process. Yeast and sugary grape juice go into the tank; yeast eats the sugar, converts it into alcohol and carbon dioxide is expelled.

Now, why does this matter to you, the dry white wine shopper? Because it tells you that the lower the ABV, the less sugar has been 'eaten' by the yeast and therefore the wine is technically sweeter. Higher ABV suggests more sugar has been converted to alcohol and that the wine will be dry (though this doesn't mean that it won't have fruity flavours and aromas, that comes down to the varietal and winemaking style). It's not a hard and fast rule, but, in a pinch, if you want an indication of whether or not the white you're considering will be dry, check the ABV. Anything in the 12% and above range should fit the category, while 10–11.5% will be semi-sweet and under 10% will be sweet. But be warned – this rule doesn't really apply to reds, which are all generally fermented to dryness, but can be fruitier and riper tasting when the alcohol level is high, or fortified wines, which have a neutral spirit added, and therefore can be sweet and boozy at the same time.

10. Don't write off an entire grape variety or region just because you got burned once

In other words, be patient and open minded. So you bought a £20 ($25) bottle of Chardonnay and didn't like it. Bummer. Instead of declaring that you 'hate Chardonnay' and writing off the varietal entirely, see what an expression from Burgundy tastes like, or California, or New Zealand. By that same token, don't let that one experience make you think that you won't ever like a Chardonnay – or any wine – from a particular region. Just because you didn't like how your Mum cooked broccoli as a child, it doesn't mean someone else hasn't worked out how to make it taste delicious, right? Do your best to take note of what wasn't working for you with that one bottle and then try to communicate that the next time you go shopping or are scanning a restaurant's wine list – what you learned from the first failed experience can lead to a successful second chance. Obviously, of course, if you try, try and try again and you're still not into it, then by all means file it in your 'This Wine May Not Be for Me' folder.

Guide to Glassware

At the risk of never getting an endorsement deal from a glassware company, I'll be honest: you don't really need any other type of wine glass beyond an all-purpose glass. Especially if you're just starting to get into wine.

I understand the sense of occasion a flute brings, and certainly appreciate and value the important aeration provided by a Burgundy bowl. But if you only get to pick one, a clear, thin-lipped, 'cut-rim' all-purpose glass should be it. It's the wine glass equivalent of the perfect pair of jeans.

The All-Purpose Glass

A stemmed glass with a U-shaped bowl that is wider at the stem and narrows slightly as it gets up to the rim.

Use it for: Literally any style of wine, if need be, but typically it's good for most whites, rosés, spicy red wines and non-Champagne sparklers.

Pros: Extremely versatile. Plus, the average-sized glass allows for closer proximity to the juice for more of an up-close-and-personal appreciation. Emphasises acidity in wines and the reduced surface area/smaller opening helps the liquid maintain a cooler temperature.

Cons: May make it more challenging to pick up on the subtleties of a particular wine that benefits from coddling and special treatment, i.e. old, rare or more expensive wines from highly prized producers and wine growing regions.

Four more to consider

The Flute

A stemmed glass with a narrow, small bowl that extends tall up to the rim. An off-shoot style of flute called a 'tulip' is becoming increasingly popular (picture an upside-down, pear-shaped bowl) thanks to its ability to better capture the aromas and flavours of sparkling wine.

Use it for: All manner of sparkling wines, except perhaps pétillant naturel wines.

Pros: Classic design that subliminally screams 'special occasion'. Also, from a technical standpoint, the shape encourages the formation of a continuous stream of bubbles (though some might argue it does this too well, letting the carbonation dissipate faster than may be desirable).

Cons: Less favoured among wine and restaurant industry types because it inhibits swirling the wine, and therefore makes deep-diving into the aromas more challenging.

The Burgundy Bowl

Essentially a fishbowl on a stem, the signature of this glass is a large, wide bowl that noticeably narrows towards the rim.

Use it for: Light-bodied, aromatic red wines, fuller-bodied white wines and skin contact (orange) wines.

Pros: The big-bowl-but-narrow-opening shape provides essential aeration, and is therefore more effective at accumulating and showing off a wine's more subtle and delicate aromas. It also helps to play up the rounder texture of fuller whites.

The Bordeaux Glass

Basically an XL version of an all-purpose glass. The bowl is larger and extends tall, tapering in just a touch at the lip of the glass.

Use it for: Medium and fuller-bodied red wines with big tannins.

Pros: By forcing more distance between your nose and the wine with its size, it helps temper the intensity of the alcohol of the typically boozy wines it's designed to hold. Also, the larger size of the glass allows the intense combination of alcohol, tannin, oak, acidity and ripe fruit in these wines to breathe and better integrate.

The Dessert Wine Glass

Like a miniature version of an all-purpose glass, these squat glasses have a shorter stem and smaller bowl that narrows at the rim

Use it for: Ports, Madeiras, sherries and all varieties of dessert wine.

Pros: Helps stunt evaporation and concentrate the high-octane dessert wines' sweet flavours and aromas. An added bonus is that these glasses are also good for tasting spirits.

Cons: Potentially not worth the extra expense considering the category is consumed less frequently.

The 'Dos' and 'Don'ts' of Storing and Serving

Storing

DO

Store open bottles of wine in the fridge: No worries if you can't finish that whole bottle from last night – as long as you cork it and keep it relatively cool, which helps slow down the spoilage process from oxygen exposure, it should last at least another day or two (maybe longer for red wine).

Find the coolest, darkest place in your house to store your wines: Aside from exposure to oxygen, heat and light are wine's greatest enemies. If you don't have the money, space or need for a wine fridge, a spot in a (not-too-dry, relatively humid) cellar, hallway or kitchen cupboard should do just fine.

Store your wine horizontally: Although somewhat of an old-school mentality – born of the days when the vast majority of wines were sealed with cork and therefore needed the contact with the wine to prevent it from drying out – it remains a solid practice. And if for no other reason, it's a more efficient, effective use of space.

DON'T

Let your wine get too hot or too cold: Store your wine anywhere that is hotter than 26°C (80°F) and it will cook, or colder than 0°C (32°F) and it will freeze or, worse, explode if it's a sparkling wine.

Expose your wine to radical temperature shifts: Imagine going from the comfortable temperature of your home to baking in a hot, humid sauna, to jumping into a near-frozen lake. Traumatising.

Serving

DO

Chill light-bodied, low-tannin, aromatic red wines: Aim for somewhere in the 10-13°C (50-55°F) range; it will make the wine taste more refreshing and help highlight fruit flavours and the brightness of a wine's acidity.

Invest in a good bottle opener: Specifically, a 'waiter's friend' (or wine key) with a double-hinge fulcrum (the metal part). The flexibility of this style will help keep you from breaking the cork. And it's not an expensive tool, either – you can generally find them for under £10 ($12) in a supermarket, cookery or wine shop.

Consider decanting your wine: Traditionally used to separate sediment off the wine in older red bottles, decanting has become more fashionable and common across the board these days. The real benefit of the process is that it gently exposes the wine to air, softening its acids and tannin, effectively smoothing out all the sharp edges and wrinkles. It can be particularly helpful in taming the funk that comes off so-called reductive wines.

Smell your glasses before you use them: As important as it is to make sure your dishware and cutlery are clean before you use them, so it goes with your glassware. One of the best, most enjoyable parts about drinking wine is appreciating its fragrance. It's best that there's no residual soap smell or dusty cupboard taint getting in the way.

Go straight through the wax on wax closures: As nice an aesthetic effect as they have, wax closures can throw a slight curve ball as far as approach goes. Best not to treat it like a traditional foil closure and instead twist the screw straight through the top without trying to remove any of it beforehand. Once the cork is halfway out, you can do a little cleanup around the rim of the bottle to ensure that no residual wax bits go into the wine when you pull it completely out.

Serving

DON'T

Serve your white wines too cold: Why? Because you'll taste less. Light-bodied, less-aromatic wines should be served colder, in the 4–8°C (40–45°F) range, whereas more expressive and fuller-bodied whites should ideally be served in the slightly-warmer-but-still-technically cold range of 8–10°C (45–50°F).

Serve your red wines too warm: Heat will exacerbate the alcohol content of a wine, making your nose hairs burn when you go in for a big whiff. Conventional wisdom generally dictates that light-to-medium bodied reds should be served around 13–15°C (55–60°F), while fuller-bodied reds are better enjoyed in the 15–20°C (60–68°F) range.

Smell the cork to verify that your wine isn't corked: Instead, smell the wine itself! Taking a quick whiff over the bottle opening will suffice. If it doesn't smell like damp cardboard or wet dog, you're good. Because, at the end of the day, even a cork that isn't tainted still smells like cork, so really how helpful is it to smell it?

Take your thumb off the cork and cage when you're opening sparkling wine: Opening a bottle of bubbly should look something like this: cut and remove the top of the foil. Put your thumb over the cage, twist open the cage tab (without taking it off), angle the bottle and rotate the base with one hand as the other wriggles the cork in the opposite direction, slowly pulling up. Keeping your hand on the cork until it's off is the best insurance policy against it violently popping off in potentially dangerous directions.

Overpour your glass: Seriously, no matter how rough the day. If the glass is too full and you try to do your best professional swirl-and-sniff, chances are you're going to end up making a mess.

Let past-its-prime, open wine go to waste: See if you can't find a recipe for a stew, or soup or sauce where it can be given a respectable second-chance at life.

Become a Better Taster:
A Face-Off Drinking Game

Here's the thing: the only way to get better at tasting wine is to taste more wine. This is not me trying to peer pressure you, it's just a fact.

A lot of the important words we use to talk about wine can seem so abstract, such as 'earthy', 'fruit-forward' or 'tannic'. As such, I find that drinking examples of opposing concepts side by side can be extremely enlightening. The following are some pairs to try together.

A Stainless Steel An Oaky White

French Chablis or Austrian Grüner Veltliner
and Chardonnay from Napa or Sonoma, USA.

French Oak New American Oak
(toast, vanilla, baking spices) (coconut, dill)

Red blend from Bordeaux,
France, and a Spanish Rioja.

A Low-Tannin A Tannic Red

Gamay from Beaujolais or Pinot Noir from France
and Nebbiolo from Barolo or Barbaresco, Italy.

A Light-Bodied A Full-Bodied Wine

For white, Muscadet from the Loire Valley and a Viognier from the Rhône.
For red, a French Pinot Noir from Burgundy and Cabernet Sauvignon from Napa.

A Low-Acid A High-Acid Wine

For white, a Côtes-du-Rhône from France, and an Albariño from Spain.
For red, a Zinfandel from California and a Barbera from Piedmont.

A Dry A Sweet White

Austrian Riesling and a
Spätlese Riesling from Germany.

A Fruit-Forward An Earthy Red

Argentinian Malbec and a Côtes-du-Rhône or Grenache,
Syrah and Mourvèdre (GSM) blend from France.

Tropical Fruit Mellow Tree Fruit
(apricot, papaya, mango) (yellow apple, pear)

Alsatian Gewürztraminer, or New Zealand
Sauvignon Blanc and Italian Pinot Grigio.

Red Fruit Black Fruit

A Pinot Noir from California, or Sangiovese from Tuscany, and a
Mourvèdre-based red from Bandol, France, or a Negroamaro from Puglia.

Fresh Fruit Dried Red
Fruit Flavours

Austrian Zweigelt and a Valpolicella Ripasso
from northeastern Italy.

Part II

White

Chardonnay

Notable Regions
Burgundy and Champagne in France, California, Oregon and Washington in the USA, New Zealand, Canada, Italy, Chile and South Africa.

Drink It With
Everything from oysters, light fish and shellfish if you're dealing with Chablis, to cream-sauced chicken with mushrooms if you're doing aged white Burgundy or Californian. Butter and cream-based sauces are your friend. Stick to seafood, chicken, veal, squash and root vegetables, and avoid anything spicy.

Say It Right: *Shar-duh-nay*

You know that friend whose personality changes based on who they're dating? That's basically Chardonnay – it's called 'the winemaker's' grape' for a reason. The comparison is not intended as an insult; without question, it's one of the most popular wine grapes in the world.

Where a grape is grown, how it's treated in the vineyard and the vision of the winemaker are always influential factors. It's just that with Chardonnay, the shapeshifting can be quite dramatic. That's why when someone throws down the hammer and exclaims, 'I hate Chardonnay', often the next question a wine professional should ask them is, 'Okay, but where was this Chardonnay you hated from? California? France? Somewhere else entirely?'. We ask this not to be condescending, but because the differences in style are so dramatically different. It's totally possible for you to dislike a 'classic' oaky-buttery Napa Chardonnay, but be in love with a white Burgundy.

That this grape is so divisive is ironic given that, on paper at least, it's got such likeable qualities. It has a plush texture, moderate acidity, mild flavours of apple, pear and citrus, and is dry without being too aggressive about it. The love-it-or-hate-it thing ultimately comes down to who the grape is in a relationship with. Chardonnay has been going out with Burgundy the longest; since at least the 17th century. Together, the two have – and continue to – produce some of the most lauded, ageworthy white wines in the world. There, the varietal shows off its skill as a chameleon of style: sometimes round, fresh and easy at the basic village level, or lean with a racy mineral-citrus thread in Chablis; at other times, it has a rich opulence with a hint of savoury in bottlings from prestige regions like Meursault, Corton-Charlemagne, Puligny-Montrachet and Pouilly-Fuissé.

For as synonymous as Chardonnay has become with the New World, they've really only been together since the 1980s when it exploded in popularity. This was a Chardonnay unlike the version we'd come to know from France. In the warmer climate of regions such as the west coast of the USA, Australia, South Africa and South America, the varietal displays more ripe tropical fruit flavours and the use of oak tends to be different, too. It's a misconception that Old World Chardonnay has nothing to do with oak – it actually does, but it presents differently. There, it's more toasted-nutty/savoury-cheesy, whereas in the New World, it has flavours of caramel, butter, vanilla and baking spices.

The grape's other strongholds include cool-climate places such as New Zealand and Canada, which produce something more acid-driven, as well as northeastern Italy, which riffs on a French style. Let's not forget Chardonnay's crucial role in the sparkling wine world. It is one of three major grapes permitted in the production of Champagne, and is similarly used in Lombardy, Italy, to produce the Champagne-method Franciacorta sparkling wine.

Sauvignon Blanc

Say It Right: *So-veen-yawn Blonk*
Other Known Aliases: *Fumé Blanc (Foo-may Blonk)*

While some may not find it easy being green, Sauvignon Blanc has made quite the successful career of it.

Frequently cast as the antithesis to Chardonnay, this lean, crisp 'wild white' varietal is one of the most important and widely planted in the world, easily identified by its characteristic greenness. Its flavour profile reads like a head-to-toe outfit homage to the hue: green fruits (lime, gooseberry, green melon, green apple, kiwi), green vegetables (pepper, asparagus, jalapeño, sugar snap peas), green herbs, green tea … and yes, you can even find hints of the colour as you admire Sauvignon Blanc in the glass.

Of the grape's many notable HQs across the wine-growing world, its native Loire Valley in France is arguably the most iconic. There, in the famed regions of Sancerre and Pouilly-Fumé, it shines as a solo artist. Typically fermented and aged in stainless steel, these pristine, sharp-edged expressions are a celebration of fresh herbs, cool, textured minerality and freshly-squeezed citrus.

Further south in Bordeaux, Sauvignon Blanc's signature zip and freshness is used in partnership with plump Sémillon to create the round, oak-aged dry whites of Entre-Deux-Mers and Graves, and, of course, the famous sweet dessert wines of Sauternes and Barsac. There's a considerable amount of it grown in the southwestern Languedoc-Roussillon, though it mostly ends up in light, tart blends, not much of which is all that exciting. Better to poke around elsewhere in Europe in areas such as Alto-Adige in northern Italy, and Styria in southeastern Austria, to find some interesting, racy, single-varietal examples.

Notable Regions
France (specifically the Loire Valley), New Zealand, Chile, South Africa, California in the USA, Australia and Italy.

Drink It With
Raw oysters; clams and mussels; prawns (shrimp); smoked salmon with crème fraîche and dill and halibut with lemon and fennel. Also, herb-heavy sauces, salads and artichokes and asparagus. Pairing with goat's cheese is also classic.

Key Words
You want a **dry, light-bodied** white that's **heavy on citrus and herbs** and a **mineral** texture; are looking for something to **pair with vegetables and seafood** or **drink on its own**; not pricey – would go to £30-40 ($40-50) for a good bottle; like **stainless steel-fermented whites**; the **opposite of Chardonnay**.

You Might Also Like
Grüner Veltliner, Verdejo, Albariño, Vermentino, Erbaluce, Vinho Verde, Txakoli and Muscadet.

Obviously, no conversation about Sauvignon Blanc would be complete without mention of New Zealand. The Marlborough region, specifically, has given Sancerre some competition with an iteration that coaxes out more tropical fruit notes (think ripe white peach and passion fruit) to add to the expected herbs and green vegetable mix.

Not surprisingly, the USA's wine-producing juggernaut, California, also has considerable stake in the Sauvignon Blanc game. Originally known there as Fumé Blanc, it's still made across Napa and Sonoma into a richer, fleshier, oak-aged style.

Riesling

Say It Right: *Ree-sling*

Notable Regions
Germany, Austria, France (specifically, Alsace), Australia, USA, Hungary and Canada.

Drink It With
Lean, dry versions work well with shellfish and counterbalance a rich butter sauce; the off-dry to sweet expressions are great with fatty cuts of meat (pork belly!), fried foods and spicy dishes; and the super-sweet stuff is dynamite with seared foie gras, hard cheeses or desserts with stone fruits and honey.

Key Words
You like citrussy, **acid-driven whites**; are a **versatile drinker**, sometimes you want something super lean, dry, and mineral, and other times you're in the mood for sweet; are looking for wines that **pair easily with food**; want to drink what the sommeliers drink.

You Might Also Like
Sylvaner, Scheurebe, dry Furmint, Txakoli, Müller-Thurgau, Albariño and Jacquère

Any actor who's ever been typecast understands Riesling's plight.

It has this impressive, well-rounded CV: one of the oldest and most important varieties in Germany; capable of producing incredibly age-worthy wines; exceptionally accomplished at expressing terroir; and, between its myriad styles, pairs with pretty much any dish or cuisine you can imagine. And yet, most of the time, when you say Riesling, the only thing people think of is something sweet, which is ironic, since the majority of Riesling made around the world is dry.

Part of the grape's PR problem stems from the fact that it has such a vibrant fruit flavour profile. Expect to find all the citrus, stone fruit, orchard fruit, and sometimes tropical fruit, in the glass at the same time. So even when it's technically fermented to dryness, the intensity of that natural cocktail can give off an impression of sweetness. It also doesn't help that for a time, a lot of what was exported was designed to be a cheap, disproportionately sweet version of itself – the cloying taste of which scarred and scared off a lot of palates.

Although many wine drinkers treat the word 'sweet' like some kind of offensive slur, in its native Germany, Riesling is celebrated for its ability to deftly slide up and down the sugar scale. At one extreme you have the searingly dry, linear *trocken* expressions, typically offering visions of citrus zest, under-ripe peach and cool river rocks. *Kabinett* and *Feinherb* represent the off-dry options. These wines are equal measures of juicy, sweet and fresh, and their lower ABV puts them in the 'delightfully swiggable' category. At the other end of the spectrum are the decidedly sweet *Spätlese* and *Auslese* styles, which see the fruit take on a lush, honeyed, buttery quality. Lastly, the nectar-of-the-gods entries featuring botrytised (otherwise known

The World's Major Riesling Styles: the Elevator Pitch Edition

Germany
Where you go to experience Riesling performing at the top level across all styles.

Austria
When you want a fuller-bodied Riesling that shoots laser beams of steely acidity.

Alsace
For dry Rieslings with weight, power and richness.

Australia and New Zealand
Are you a fan of sucking on lemons and limes? Great.

New York State and Washington
The American-accented version of what Germany does.

Canada
Try their super-sweet icewine version.

as 'Noble Rot'; see page 160) grapes: *Beerenauslese* and *Trockenbeerenauslese*. (Nerdy sidebar: again, it's worth noting that the terms for the sweeter styles technically don't refer to the sugar content in the wine but rather the ripeness level of the grapes at harvest.) The varietal's success as a sweet wine hinges on it being a natural powerhouse of acidity. It's what keeps even the sweetest styles from tasting syrupy. Not to mention that it helps the wines have such long lifespans. And on that note, here's a fun fact: sweet expressions will taste less so the longer they're aged, to the point where a 30-year-old Auslese Riesling might taste practically dry.

Beyond Germany, Riesling's other two major European bases are Austria and Alsace, France. In the former, it's made almost exclusively in a dry style that's generally characterised as being slightly fuller bodied, a little spicy, and having a cutting, razor-sharp acidity. Alsace's prized Rieslings, while also mostly dry (some noble rot-infected grapes are used to make dessert wines) display a more rich, robust personality with distinctive mineral tones. In addition to that, Australian Rieslings from the Barossa, Eden and Clare Valleys are some of the driest you'll ever come across.

Chenin Blanc

Say It Right: *Shen-in Blonk*
Other Known Aliases: *Steen*

We've all taken one of those generic personality tests in which a series of multiple-choice questions is supposed to be able to accurately typecast you. You know, 'Please tick Box A if you're this way, Box B if you're that, or Box C if you're some other way entirely'. Chenin Blanc is the kind of grape that looks at that test, laughs, ticks all three boxes and then goes on about its business.

It's one of those rare, exception-to-the-rule varietals that is not just produced in a range of styles – dry, off-dry, dessert, sparkling, oxidative and fortified – but is actually praised for its proficiency in all of them.

Chenin Blanc is best known for extending its full range of motion in the middle of the Loire Valley, France. Its dry whites from the sub-regions of Vouvray, Saumur and Anjou are marked by flavours of apple, melon and pear, a punchy grapefruit-lemon acidity, and a unique undertone of white flowers, raw honey and hay. Its fine-beaded, frothy sparklings follow a similar flavour profile, but will frequently offer additional notes of toasted nuts and yeasty raw dough. These will either be produced under the regionally broad label, Crémant de Loire, or Vouvray, if made there specifically. Some of the most unique, 'geeky' expressions come from the sub-region of Savennières. In this mini-mecca for biodynamic winemaking, the grape is often treated in an oxidative style (i.e. exposed to oxygen during the winemaking process) that helps coax out a smorgasbord of complex flavours and textures: earthy, oily, mineral, woolly, nutty, bruised orchard fruit. And what's more, these wines seem to only get more interesting with age. Of course, let's not forget Chenin's crowning achievement in the region: those late-harvest, botrytised sweet wines that taste like ripe, gingered peaches, apples and quince that have been dipped in honey and skewered with a vibrant bolt of citrus. To find these, keep an eye

Notable Regions
Loire Valley, France, South Africa, Argentina, California and Washington state, USA.

Drink it With
Dry and sparkling versions work with lemon-driven preparations of chicken and seafood, fried foods, and creamy sauces; off-dry ones favor boldly spiced Asian and Middle Eastern dishes; and pair sweet expressions with apple/pear or almond-based desserts and rich, savoury ingredients.

Key Words
You like **light-bodied** wines with **bold aromatics**; are into slap-you-in-the-face **bright acidity**; appreciate honeyed, nutty flavours; like dry whites, sparkling and sweet dessert wines.

You Might Also Like
Dry Riesling, Soave, Fiano, sous-voile Chardonnay or Savagnin from the Jura, Kabinett Riesling and Scheurebe from Germany for demi-sec; sweet Tokaji for dessert wine.

out for small 187 ml bottles (warning: it's going to be pricey stuff for the quantity) that are labelled Vouvray moelleux, or come from the sub-regions of Coteaux de Layon, Quarts de Chaume and Bonnezeaux.

Outside of the Loire Valley, Chenin shows off fewer of its multiple personalities. In South Africa, where it is the most widely planted variety in the country, Chenin has historically been produced as either a base wine destined to be distilled into brandy, or as a filler grape for blends. Increasingly, it's being treated with more attention and care, largely made in a lean, dry, citrus-and-mineral-forward style, though some warmer-climate expressions take on a riper, more concentrated quality. The grape's other stomping ground of note is California, USA, where, after being treated as nothing more than characterless swill in the 1970s and 1980s, it has experienced a recent resurgence among new, young producers committed to making it into a quality dry wine.

Sémillon

Say It Right: *Sem-ee-yawn*

Notable Regions
France (specifically Bordeaux), Australia, California and Washington state in the USA, South Africa, Chile and Argentina.

Drink It With
If it's dry – oily smoked fish; chicken or pork with fruit; seafood stews. If it's sweet – foie gras and rich pâtés; baked fruit desserts; cheeses such as Roquefort and aged Cheddar.

Key Words
Dry: You like **fuller-bodied, not too acidic** wines with an **herbal quality**. Sweet: You **appreciate ripe orchard fruit flavours** with a **honeyed edge**.

You Might Also Like
Viura, Garganega and Friulano if you like it dry; if you like it sweet, try late-harvest Riesling from Germany or Austria, sweet Tokaji, Sélection de Grains Nobles (SGN) of Riesling, Muscat or Pinot Gris from Alsace, Vouvray Moelleux and Quarts de Chaume.

When it comes to wine grapes, being a star doesn't necessarily mean you're going to be a household name. Often, the fame and acclaim go to the wine (or its associated region) and not the grape(s) from which it's made; one of those classic 'the whole is greater than the sum of its parts' situations. Which is why Sauternes – one of the most well-known and revered dessert wines in the world – probably rings a bell, but Sémillon does not.

As a single varietal, this unsung hero tends to produce round, full-bodied whites with a mellow citrussy-peachy tinge (read: low-acid), and aromatics that range from beeswax and wool to honey, white flowers and green figs. When made in a less-ripe expression, it could very well act as a Sauvignon Blanc understudy, offering a bit more mouth-watering green apple and grapefruit tang, and a nose of wild green herbs. All that being said, Sémillon's work as a solo artist is rarely the point. Aside from some few-and-far-between examples in places such as California and Washington state, USA, and South Africa, the grape's only real notable stand-alone performance comes from southern Australia's Hunter Valley. There, it's famously produced in a low-alcohol, high-acid, dry style that's designed for aging and is prized for the signature toasty-roasted, nutty flavour it develops.

Otherwise, Sémillon's greatest hits come from its roles in group acts. Without question, the grape's most important growing region is Bordeaux, in southwestern France, where it has long been partnered with Sauvignon Blanc to make some pretty exceptional dry and sweet whites. As far as dry whites are concerned, their partnership most commonly lives under the label of Bordeaux Blanc. At their simplest, these wines are a great, anytime-of-the-week option for dry white wine drinkers who prefer a fuller texture and appreciate good value. But they achieve their fullest potential in the

Sauternes Alternatives

For those occasions when you don't necessarily want to splurge on Sauternes, change-your-life-delicious though it may be, look for the more affordable Sémillon-based dessert wines from the neighbouring regions of Montbazilliac, Cadillac, Loupiac and Cerons.

Pessac-Léognan sub-region, where, with the influence of oak and age, they are transformed into best-in-show beauties with an intoxicating combination of smoky, tropical fruit, beeswax, wet wool and a slick, oily texture.

In these dry Bordeaux whites (and their New World imitators), the Sémillon to Sauvignon Blanc ratio slides the scale. But in what is arguably their most iconic collaboration, it is Sémillon that takes centre stage. The thin-skinned grape is highly susceptible to botrytis, the coveted strain of so-called 'noble rot' responsible for making grapes raisinate, concentrating their sugars and sweet fruit flavours. As such, Sémillon typically makes up the lion's share of the blend – usually 4:1 – in the honeyed, lush, zesty dessert wine, Sauternes. It's also worth mentioning that the dessert wines of Barsac, a sub-region of Sauternes, are equally fantastic, slightly lighter in body and with a punchier acidity.

Gewürztraminer

Say It Right: *Guh-vertz-trah-meener*

If you've ever been smacked in the face by the perfume of someone who doesn't know when to stop spritzing, then you have a pretty good sense of what it's like to stick your nose in a glass of Gewürztraminer. It's heady stuff, with loud, distinctive aromatics that are all too eager to leap out and grab your attention. Lychee! Rose petals! Guava! Tangerine! Grapefruit! Apricot! Peach! Pineapple! Allspice! Incense! Ginger! Honey! Looking for a good gateway grape to start practising blind tasting with? Gewürtz, as it's 'more simply' called, is the one

Like anything with a big personality, the reaction to the wines made from this grape tend to be love it or hate it. That being said, you'll certainly find a lot of love for Gewürtz in Alsace, arguably the grape's most important growing region. In this northeastern corner of France they've even gone so far as to anoint it 'noble grape' status (along with Riesling, Pinot Gris and Muscat), meaning it can be planted on the region's Grand Cru vineyards (aka the best sites). It is from these sites that the gold-standard expression of the grape is produced. Outside of Alsace, you're likely to find the wines of this cool climate-loving grape in the neighbouring Pfalz region of Germany, Italy's Alto Adige, where it is alleged to have originated from, Austria, New Zealand and Northern California and Oregon in the USA.

Now, it's easy to read through that list of Gewürtz's very tropical-leaning fruit characteristics and automatically pigeonhole it as a sweet wine. Wrong. Well, sort of. In Alsace, in special years when the growing conditions are just right, it can be used to make two types of highly prized – read devastatingly delicious and quite pricey – dessert wines called Vendanges Tardives and Sélection de Grains Nobles (VT and SGN, for short). But the truth of the matter is, the majority of Gewürztraminers are fermented to dryness. While the sweet smell of various fruits may be there, the

Notable Regions
France (specifically Alsace), Germany, Italy, Austria, New Zealand, Northern California, Oregon and New York state's Finger Lakes region in the USA.

Drink It With
Asian, Middle Eastern and Indian cuisines, the more complex the heat and spice profile the better (read: bring on tagines and curries); soft cow's milk cheeses; smoked meat (duck, pork, beef) and fish such as salmon and trout.

Key Words
You like **richer, fuller-bodied, fruit-forwards** whites; are not afraid of **floral aromatics** or a little sweetness; **don't need a lot of puckery acidity** in your wine.

You Might Also Like
Muscat, Torrontes, Alsatian Pinot Gris, warm-climate Viognier, Jurançon, Hárslevelü and Moschofilero (if you want something floral but on the drier, leaner side).

sugar in the initial grape juice has almost entirely been converted to alcohol.

The admittedly tricky thing with Gewürtz is that because it's a fuller-bodied grape without a lot of natural acidity to counteract its richer, oilier texture, these wines often taste a little sweeter than they technically are. It's a quality that perhaps makes it a little intense to drink on its own, but dynamite with spicy, boldly flavoured Asian food (think Thai, Vietnamese, Szechuan and Indonesian).

Notable Regions
France (specifically the Rhône Valley), California, Washington and Oregon in the USA and Australia.

Drink It With
Roast chicken or grilled pork; shellfish like lobster and crab (or crab cakes!) served with a rich, buttery sauce; oily, silver-skinned fish (eel, mackerel, sardines) and smoked fish (salmon, trout) would be a good texture match, as well as something meaty, such as swordfish; risotto and baked or roasted preparations of squash.

Key Words
You like white wines with **richness**, weight and a not-so-subtle amount of booze; think that a wine with a **waxy texture** sounds interesting; think acidity belongs in more of a background role; prefer **ripe tree fruit** flavours and the smell of white flowers.

You Might Also Like
Viognier, richer expressions of Chardonnay and Grenache Blanc.

Marsanne and Roussanne

Say It Right: *Mar-sahn and Roo-sahn*

Marsanne and Roussanne don't just have a good, solid working relationship, they're besties. Akin to a together-all-the-time, can't-talk-about-one-without-mentioning-the-other type of closeness. The kind of friends that complement and bring out the best in one another, like macaroni and cheese, or jam and clotted cream.

The dynamic duo's most renowned collaborations can be found in the northern half of France's Rhône Valley. Although the area is better known for its Syrah-based reds, the towns of Saint Joseph, Hermitage and Crozes-Hermitage dedicate a small percentage of their production to whites made from a blend of the two grapes. These rare wines tend to be fuller-bodied, with an opulent, borderline oily texture and notes of ripe tree fruits (apple, pear, quince), honey, honeysuckle and almond.

Marsanne, being the more vigorous grower of the two, often makes up the lion's share of the blend, contributing weight, alcohol and a deep golden-yellow colour to the wine. Roussanne's part is admittedly smaller, but by no means insignificant. The more delicate varietal, it has a naturally higher acidity, providing much needed lift and freshness to the blend, and is also spicier and more aromatic, often lending a fragrance of alpine herbs and white flowers. Also in the Rhône, the pair teams up to make the nutty, brioche-y sparkling wine from Saint-Péray, and contributes to the blend for white Côtes-du-Rhône.

Forced to single one out as more independent, you'd probably have to go with Marsanne, if for no other reason than its ability to grow easily has contributed to a larger body of work outside of the partnership. You can find it everywhere from Provence's Cassis region

(unique for producing more white wine than rosé) to Switzerland, where it's used to make both dry and sweet wines, as well as California in the USA and the Victoria region of Australia. Roussanne, meanwhile, has the distinction of being one of only 13 grapes allowed to be included in the prized wines of the southern Rhône's Châteauneuf-du-Pape region. It is also made in very small amounts as a single varietal wine in Savoie, in eastern France, as well as in California and Oregon in the USA. Of course, that being said, many of these other regions – namely Australia and USA – will end up reuniting the bosom buddies in Rhône-inspired blends.

Pinot Gris

Say It Right: *Pee-no Gree*
Other Known Aliases: Pinot Grigio *(Pee-no Gree-jee-oh)*, Grauburgunder *(Gr-ow-berr-gun-der)*

Wine and the property market (real estate) have a lot in common. With both, it's amazing to see just how much location can alter your perspective and define your expectations. The same-size, same-price flat will no doubt look very different from one city – or even simply one neighbourhood – to another. Much in the same way, ordering an Italian Pinot Grigio is going to be a very different experience from ordering a Pinot Gris from Alsace or Oregon, despite the fact that, genetically speaking, they're all made from the same grape.

In France, this pink-skinned, white mutation of Pinot Noir (confusing, I know) does its best-known work in Alsace. There, the 'noble' varietal produces fuller-bodied, plush whites that deliver flavours of ultra-ripe peach/apricot/nectarine, a balancing lemon acidity and a subtle flash of smoke and spice. In top years, you'll see some of it reserved for the production of the region's prized late-harvest dessert wines: Vendanges Tardives and Sélection de Grains Nobles. Think of the flavours of the dry style on steroids, layered with honey and wrapped with a rich, buttery bow, and you get an idea of what makes these intense sweet wines such a treat.

While Germany, Switzerland and Hungary tend to follow Alsace's stylistic direction, producing either full, fruit-forward dry whites or sweet wines (or both), Italy has envisioned an entirely different identity for Pinot Gris. As Pinot Grigio, it presents as an almost unrecognisable version of its French or German self. Instead of round and voluptuous, it's light and lean; the characteristic flavour of mature stone fruit is replaced with mellow, muted tones of citrus, melon and apple, and instead of a bold, love-it-or-hate-it personality, its wines are generally easy and neutral. Production of the grape is largely concentrated in the northeastern part of the country.

Notable Regions
Alsace in France, Italy, Germany, Hungary, Switzerland, California and Oregon, USA.

Drink It With
If you're drinking Italian expressions, go for light dishes: pan-fried or steamed white fish and shellfish; salads. With the riper versions, you can play with bolder flavours: roasted and fried chicken or fish; cured meats; smoked cheeses and spicy dishes.

Key Words
Pinot Grigio drinkers, you like **dry, light-bodied, neutral whites** with nice acidity and **soft, slightly peachy flavours**; want something you can **drink on its own** without food. If you're a fan of the Alsatian style, you're more open to **juicier tree and stone fruit** and some **floral notes**.

You Might Also Like
For the lighter style, try Trebbiano, Arneis and Vernaccia, or Alsatian Pinot Blanc, Verdejo and Chasselas for something fuller.

The regions of Veneto and Lombardy mostly churn out high volumes of inexpensive and inoffensive expressions, while in Alto Adige and Friuli Venezia Giulia, you can find more characterful, complex, small-production versions.

Over in the New World, Pinot Gris has made quite a name for itself in Oregon, USA, where it is the most planted varietal in the state. Here, it tends to produce medium-bodied dry wines that fall somewhere between an Alsatian and Italian style, and are generally presented as a more aromatic, fruit-driven alternative to Chardonnay. And in other places where it's popular, such as New Zealand or California, USA, you use the producer's choice of grape name as an indicator of the style of wine: Pinot Grigio if it's on the lighter-brighter end, and Pinot Gris if it's fuller, riper and more aromatic.

Pinot Blanc

Notable Regions
Northeastern France
(Alsace, Moselle),
Luxembourg,
northeastern Italy,
Germany, Austria,
Hungary, Slovenia,
Canada and Oregon,
in the USA.

Drink It With
Lightly sauced white
fish and shellfish; simple
omelettes and quiches;
roasted chicken or
chicken salad sandwiches
and vegetables.

Key Words
You like **easy, neutral
white** wines; don't want
too much acid, body
or fruit flavour.

You Might Also Like
Basic-level French
Chardonnay (Bourgogne
Blanc, Mâcon-Villages
or Beaujolais Blanc),
Verdicchio, Sylvaner,
Oregon Pinot Gris
and California
Sauvignon Blanc.

Say It Right: *Pee-no Blonk*
Other Known Aliases: Weissburgunder *(Vice-burg-under)*,
Pinot Bianco *(Pee-no Bee-ahn-ko)*

Think of Pinot Blanc as the mini-van of varietals: the safe bet you pick for its utility and affordability.

A white mutation of Pinot Noir, the grape is often described in very middle-of-the-road terms. It's light to medium-bodied, dry, with a mellow acidity and round, soft flavours of apple, pear and white peach. More often than not, it's presented as a kind of basic, less ambitious option for fans of unoaked Chardonnay. Even its best-known wines rarely get more than a modest applause. In Alsace, it makes a lot of easy, still whites and is an important component in the blend for the region's Champagne-method sparkling wine (aka *Crémant d'Alsace*). But it hardly competes in the same league as wines made from Riesling, Gewürztraminer and Pinot Gris. You can also find significant amounts of it in the northeastern Italian regions of Friuli Venezia Giulia and Alto Adige, where it is known as Pinot Bianco. Here again, it is made in a light, Chardonnay style, or blended with Chardonnay to make sparkling wine.

In Germany, Weissburgunder is treated with a little more respect. In addition to being made in the dry, tart style, it is also being produced as a riper expression with light oak aging to add complexity. And in Austria, beyond making crisp whites, the susceptible-to-botrytis varietal is also behind some exceptional sweet wines.

And if nothing else, it's prolific, also being grown in Luxembourg, Switzerland, Hungary, Slovenia and the USA.

Viognier

Say It Right: *Vee-own-yay*

I know the song says not to call it a comeback, but when you're a grape that goes from near extinction 50 years ago to becoming so trendy that you're now planted throughout the wine-growing world, what other possible word is there for it?

Drink It With
Rich, heavily sauced dishes, because it has the weight and texture to handle it. Think fish, shellfish or white meats served with butter and cream sauces. Also plays nicely with heat and spice, so try it with an Indian or Thai-style curry.

The varietal is known for producing high-alcohol, full-fleshed wines with moderate acidity, a unique oily texture and potent aromatics that range from ripe peach and apricot to orange rind, roses and herbal spice. Today, it is grown throughout the Rhône and the Languedoc-Roussillon in France, where it is featured in white blends alongside Marsanne, Roussanne, Grenache Blanc, Bourboulenc and Vermentino. But the best expressions come from the tiny, historic appellations of Condrieu and Château-Grillet in northern Rhône. And it is the striking personality of these wines that deserves much of the credit for piquing interest.

Key Words
You want a rich, full-bodied white wine and can appreciate an **oiler texture**; you like whites with **bold aromatics**, but more specifically, you're into a **floral bouquet**.

Over in the USA, it was the Rhône wine enthusiasts in central California that were the most notable early adopters, experimenting with it not only on its own and in white blends, but also as a colour and texture-enhancing minor addition to Syrah reds (a practice borrowed from some northern Rhône producers). The technique is also popular in Australia, although the grape is also vinified on its own into a more tropical-fruited version of its floral self. Otherwise, you can find renditions from New Zealand, Chile, Argentina and South Africa, as well as some unique examples coming out of Italy's Piedmont and Tuscany.

You Might Also Like
Fuller expressions of Chardonnay, full-bodied white Riojas, Gewürztraminer (for fans of the Australian style), Torrontes, Muscat (if you're into its floral side) and Marsanne/Roussanne blends.

Albariño

Notable Regions
Spain (specifically Rias
Baixas), Portugal and
California in the USA.

Drink It With
Seafood, duh. So much
could work: ceviches
and crudos; pan-seared
scallops or a white fish
fillet dressed with lemon
and good olive oil;
steamed lobster; clams
steamed with garlic and
herbs or linguine alla
vongole; cold seafood
salad; oysters on the
half shell and brandade
tartine. Vinaigrette-
dressed salads and grilled
green vegetables would
also be a great match.

Key Words
You like **lean,
light-bodied** whites; *love*
acidity; appreciate the
mouth-watering effect
of **salinity**; are looking
for **something (not too
expensive)** to drink as an
apéritif or with seafood.

You Might Also Like
Sauvignon Blanc,
Assyrtiko, Vinho Verde,
Grüner Veltliner,
Muscadet, Jacquère,
Txakoli and
Austrian Riesling.

Say It Right: *Alba-reen-yo*
Other Known Aliases: Alvarinho *(Alva-reen-yo)*

Most would be offended at being called out for having
a 'salty' personality. But, in the case of Albariño, not
only is the adjective not intended as a character flaw,
it's actually one of the varietal's biggest selling points.

Native to northwestern Portugal, the grape is still
important there. While some single varietal examples
exist, it's mostly featured as a second-string player in
the light, naturally spritzy dry white blends of Vinho
Verde. Where Albariño has really made a name for
itself, however, is across the border in Rias Baixas. In this
northwesternmost corner of coastal Spain, the grape is
famous for producing vibrant, fresh, slightly floral whites
that evoke a kind of lemon-grapefruit-honeydew melon
punch that's been spiked with minerally salt water.

It's precisely this signature saline quality that makes
it such a perfect, mouth-watering apéritif wine and
so devastatingly good with simple preparations of just-
caught seafood (à la 'grows together, goes together'
methodology). Not to mention generally affordability
in relation to quality has made it even more endearing.
To experience the top, most 'serious' versions of Albariño,
look for the words *'cepas vellas'* on the label, which
indicates that the wine is produced from grapes
grown on older vines – more than 200 years old in
some cases.

The growing popularity of this varietal has inspired
producers in American regions such as California and
Oregon to try their hand at producing it in both
traditional and non-traditional versions.

Grüner Veltliner

Notable Regions
Austria, Slovakia, Czech Republic, New Zealand (specifically Central Otago) and Oregon and California in the USA.

Drink It With
Chicken and pork (especially done schnitzel-style); shellfish and white fish; nigiri-style sushi; green vegetables, (even asparagus!); preparations influenced by citrus and pepper; and for fuller, riper expressions try Thai and Indian cuisine.

Key Words
You like **light-bodied, lean** whites with crisp acidity; enjoy **citrus, spice, green veggie** and herb flavours; are a **fan of screw-top wines** and want something friendly that goes with just about anything for just about anyone.

You Might Also Like
Sauvignon Blanc, Albariño, Muscadet, Vermentino, dry Riesling, Aligoté, Vinho Verde and Erbaluce, Muscadet, Jacquère, Txakoli and Austrian Riesling.

Say It Right: *Groo-ner Velt-lee-ner*

Most of the time we talk about a grape as being the most valuable player (MVP) of some (relatively) small, specific sub-region: Chardonnay and Pinot Noir in Burgundy, Pinot Grigio in Friuli, Cabernet Sauvignon in Napa or Bordeaux. But, in Austria, Grüner Veltliner is the nationwide superstar.

Obviously, it's not the only white grape planted in the country; varietals such as Sauvignon Blanc, Weissburgunder (Pinot Blanc), Gelber Muskateller (Yellow Muscat) and Furmint also grow there. Not to mention their Rieslings rank among the best in the world. Still, the blunt fact remains that Grüner is Austria's most widely planted varietal – and that's accounting for both white and red – making up literally a third of the country's vineyard acreage. It's a big deal.

The irony, of course, is that for as big of a star as Grüner is in its homeland, it wasn't until fairly recently – say, within the last three decades – that the rest of the world really started to fall for its charms. For example, in some instances, it's easy, light and crisp, impossible not to like, and in others, intense, complex and rich.

Grüner is also remarkably food-friendly, thanks to its compelling mix of tangy citrus, apple, melon and pear flavours, a cutting, stony mineral edge, and a distinctive floral, white pepper and green vegetal vibe (peas, herbs and rocket (arugula) often come to mind).

It's comfortable on the table with just about anything: from a spread of sushi, to fried foods (schnitzel and spaetzle if you're going for the hometown favourite), or perhaps even spicy Asian cuisine or a rich stew if you're opting for a riper expression of the grape. And, for the record, it's also one of the few wines that's thought of as a successful match with that ever-so-challenging-to-pair vegetable, asparagus.

Style Indicator

Most Austrian Grüner follows the same model: light, dry, with a bright citrus acidity and peppery bite. Assume that those in one-litre bottles with a screw or bottle top closure are on the less complex side, intended for no-frills, everyday drinking. If it has a cork closure, it's probably a more 'serious', expensive expression (think single vineyard from a prestigious producer) and is a good candidate for aging and special occasions. Though that is not to say that high-quality Grüner cannot be found under a screw top; it is the primary closure of choice in the region.

Most of Austria's 'top' Grüners come from the sub-regions of Kremstal, Kamptal, Traisental and the Wachau. Of those, the Wachau is the boss. Its wines (which are more expensive) have unique style classifications. *Steinfeder* for the light, electric-acid Grüners, Federspiel for the dry, refined, and medium-bodied expressions, and *Smaragd* for those that, while technically still dry, are more ripe, opulent and complex.

On top of it all, not only are the leaner, more acid-driven styles an excellent 'other white meat' option when you've maxed-out on Sauv Blanc, but in general, the grape tends to deliver great value for the quality. Plus, the vast majority are bottled with a screw-top closure, so don't stress if you forgot to bring your opener to the picnic – did I mention it's a great picnic wine?

Muscat

Say It Right: *Muss-kat*
Other Known Aliases: Moscato *(Mo-skah-toe)*,
Moscatel *(Moss-ka-tell)*, Muskateller *(Moose-ka-teller)*,
Zibbibo *(Zee-bee-bo)*

It may not get the attention or mass-market recognition of an industry darling like Sauvignon Blanc or Chardonnay but, make no mistake, Muscat is an OG in the world of wine grapes. In fact, with a history that dates back to the ancient civilisations and thought to be the first domesticated grape, most would probably call it the Original Gangster.

The first thing to know about Muscat is that it isn't simply a one-man show; the name actually refers to an entire posse of grapes. Of the hundreds of different strains that fall under the Muscat umbrella, the best known and most well travelled is Muscat Blanc à Petit Grains. A bit of a Renaissance man, it's produced in a wide range of styles across the wine-growing world. In northeastern Italy, for example, it's famously made into the sweet, delicately effervescent wine known as Moscato d'Asti. It functions similarly in the northern Rhône, where it is blended with Clairette to make the fruity sparkling Clairette de Die. While in places such as Germany and Austria, it's presented as a dry, still white. And yet in Greece, southern France, other parts of Italy and Portugal, it's transformed into sweet and fortified wines.

Dessert wine is a popular vocation among the Muscat siblings, which tend to share an intense aromatic profile of ripe stone fruits, white flowers, sweet citrus and fresh grapes (a flavour surprisingly uncommon in wine-producing varietals). Muscat of Alexandria is particularly famous for its renditions in Sicily, as well as in parts of Spain, Portugal, Greece and California, USA. Interestingly in Chile, the variety is used to make the base wine that is eventually distilled into Pisco, the country's national spirit. Although its reach isn't as wide,

Notable Regions
France, Germany, Italy,
Greece, Spain, Portugal,
Austria, Germany, USA
and Australia.

Drink It With
Desserts and pastries
with fresh, dried or
roasted fruits, nuts,
caramel or honey; dark
chocolate; foie gras; a
cheese platter with aged
Cheddar, Gouda and
stinky blues.

Key Words
You like **light-to-
medium-bodied**, highly
aromatic whites that
deliver a **wallop of fruit
and floral flavours**; are
cool with sweet wines,
or even wines that smell
like sweet fruit.

You Might Also Like
Gewürztraminer,
Torrontés, Alsatian Pinot
Gris, Müller-Thurgau
and Malvasia.

Muscat Ottonel is another significant one to know. While it does the expected sweet wine thing in Lower Austria, Hungary and Romania, it's better recognised for the heady dry to off-dry whites it produces in Alsace.

It's also worth mentioning that Muscat isn't an exclusively white-skinned varietal. A red mutation of Muscat à Petit Grains, (unfortunately) called Brown Muscat is the grape behind Liqueur Muscat, a super-sweet, dark fortified wine from Australia. And there's also Muscat of Hamburg, the almost black-coloured strain used to make dessert wines in California and in small pockets across Europe.

Trebbiano

Notable Regions
France, Italy, Portugal and South America.

Drink It With
Simply prepared seafood dishes; crudité; mild washed-rind cheeses; simple green salads dressed in light vinaigrette.

Key Words
You're looking for an **easy** white with a mellow, **middle-of-the-road personality**; not too particular, you just want something that is **dry, not too heavy or acidic and inexpensive**.

You Might Also Like
Pinot Blanc, Verdicchio, basic-level unoaked French Chardonnay and Friulano.

Say It Right: *Treb-EE-ah-no*
Other Known Aliases: Ugni Blanc *(Oo-nee Blonk)*

If nothing else, you have to give it up to Trebbiano for crushing it as an everyday hero. The grape (of which there are several strains) rarely gets any mention or attention, but that does not mean its role in the wine industry is insignificant.

The most prolific of the grape's many varieties is Trebbiano Toscano. While you have probably never heard of it – or maybe just once or twice in passing – the varietal is actually responsible for producing more wine than any other in the world. Of course, the unfortunate reality of this fact is that a lot of the light, neutral, tart and generally not-that-exciting wine it makes is either distilled or processed. In France, under the pseudonym Ugni Blanc, it is used as a major (if not solo) component in the base wine that eventually becomes Cognac and Armagnac. And in northeastern Italy, juice from the freshly harvested grapes is used, often with the red wine grape Lambrusco, to produce the region's signature balsamic vinegars.

Even in its strictly wine-only roles, Trebbiano mostly plays a fade-into-the-background part. In southwestern France and throughout central and northeastern Italy, it's nothing more than a chorus member in leagues of fresh, easy and unassuming white blends. That being said, if you do happen to be interested in seeing what the grape can achieve on its own, the best examples can be found from some serious-minded producers in Abruzzo.

Notable Regions
Greece (specifically Santorini) and Australia.

Drink It With
Light, simple, citrus-driven seafood dishes (white fish and all manner of shellfish, especially); fried fish; pasta with a light cream-based sauce; raw summer vegetable salads; salty, creamy cheeses such as feta.

Key Words
You like **lean, dry, lighter-bodied** white wines with a **citrus and mineral backbone; coastal and island white wines**; are not afraid to go out on a limb and try a grape you haven't heard of before.

You Might Also Like
Chablis, Muscadet, Pigato, Austrian Riesling, Soave, Vermentino, Albariño, Txakoli and Vinho Verde.

Assyrtiko

Say It Right: *Ah-seer-tee-ko*

Overcoming a stigma can be a long, challenging and arduous road for a wine. Just ask Riesling. In this case, however, it's not so much that Assyrtiko specifically has had to fight to earn people's respect, but rather that Greek wines in general haven't been taken all that seriously.

The upturned nose brush-off stems from a period of time several decades ago when the only Greek wine people outside of the country were familiar with was Retsina. Basically, this ancient style of white wine, which is fermented with Aleppo pine tree resin and gives off an, err, 'distinctive', aroma of turpentine, didn't exactly help Greek wine win any popularity contests – especially since the pungency of the style had long been used to try and mask the flavour of poorly made wine. Long story short: it didn't work. While the divisive style is supposedly on the verge of a comeback, the point is that wine drinkers today do actually have a growing interest and appreciation for Greek wines, and that credit goes to Assyrtiko.

Native to the island of Santorini, Assyrtiko has essentially become the gateway grape of Greek wines, and it's pretty easy to understand why. Just consider the sales pitch: it's a lean, dry white with fierce waves of lemon-lime-tart apple acidity, smoky, volcanic rock minerality and a refreshing sea breeze salinity. To summarise: a Chablis that's gone on vacation to a Mediterranean island (and, on average, much less expensive than its French doppelgänger, even the top bottlings).

Though mostly intended to be enjoyed as a young, fresh wine, several of the grape's best winemakers are also experimenting with producing the grape in an age-worthy style, taking on a little more heft and savoury characteristics.

For the most part, Assyrtiko doesn't have a life outside of Santorini. And, I mean, have you seen the place? I get why you might not want to. Still, it's ability to retain its vibrant acidity in warmer climates has resulted in a number of Greece's mainland producers bringing the grape over to work with.

Interestingly, the grape has just recently been successfully produced by one of the better-known winemakers in Australia's Clare Valley. So who knows, perhaps more trips abroad await in Assyrtiko's future.

Melon de Bourgogne

Say It Right: *Mell-ahn duh Boor-goyn*

In the world of wine, it's rare for a grape to be produced in a single region, for a singular purpose. But indeed, if Melon de Bourgogne was a pony, then making the crisp, mineral, soft-personality whites of Muscadet is its one big trick.

Though the grape appears to have originated somewhere near Burgundy (hence the 'Bourgogne'), it was never exactly a hometown hero. It wasn't until it landed in the western Loire Valley that the grape 'found itself', so to speak. Never one to be the loudest voice in the room, this simple, fresh, briny white developed an identity and reputation based largely on its neutrality. Light in pretty much every way a wine can be – in body, fruitiness and alcohol – its flavour profile is characterised by mellow notes of apple and pear, hints of green herbs and white flowers and a very-reflective-of-place wet stones and seashells vibe.

To take a positive stance, you could argue that this kind of vinous blank canvas is exactly what makes Melon de Bourgogne such a successful partner with raw oysters and simply prepared seafood, letting the food be the star. Still, its mild-mannered tone (coupled with its very friendly price-point) has, historically, been somewhat detrimental, meaning it was taken less seriously.

More recently, however, the wine has been a darling of the wine nerd community, who champion the complexity of its textures and its ability to convey a sense of place. It's even starting to get credit as a moderately age-worthy white.

Look to the sub-region of Muscadet Sèvre-et-Maine to experience the top expressions, and pay attention to labels with the words *'sur lie'* on them. The term indicates that the wine was aged on the lees (dead yeast cells leftover from the fermentation process, not as gruesome

Notable Regions
Western Loire Valley (specifically Muscadet) and Oregon in the USA.

Drink It With
Raw oysters (literally their most match-made-in-heaven partner aside from Champagne); simple, light preparations of seafood and shellfish and traditional nigiri and sashimi.

Key Words
You're looking for something to pair with seafood and you want to keep the price-point reasonable; want something **light, dry and friendly** that has strong **citrus and mineral** tones.

You Might Also Like
Aligoté, Pinot Blanc, Verdicchio, Grüner Veltliner, Friulano, Pigato and Txakoli.

as it sounds), which can help boost flavour and texture.

And, lest I be called a liar, it's worth mentioning that Melon has actually done some very limited travelling outside of the Loire in recent years. Seek out some bottlings from Oregon, USA, to experience an out-of-its-element expression of the grape.

Part III

Red

Cabernet Sauvignon

Notable Regions
France (specifically Bordeaux), Chile, California (specifically Napa and Sonoma) and Washington state in the USA, Australia, Spain, Italy and South Africa.

Drink It With
Butter-based prime cut of steak or herb-crusted lamb; burgers (or Portobello burgers); red meat with warming spices, especially stews, and aged blue cheeses.

Say It Right: *Cab-er-nay So-veen-yawn*

Like James Bond, there's something very 'guys want to be him, girls want to be with him' about Cabernet Sauvignon. Sounds silly, but it really has got that level of style, swagger and celebrity.

Even if you know next to nothing about wine, you've at least heard of Cabernet Sauvignon. It's the most widely planted grape in the world – and that includes both red and white – and is responsible for some of the industry's most legendary, revered wines. Everything about its personality exudes confidence and commands attention: an unapologetically bold, full-bodied texture; intensely concentrated fruit; a firm tannic structure that fits it like a well-cut suit, and seductive, dark, broody aromatics that make you want to linger over the glass. And as if all that weren't enough of a selling point, add longevity and ageability to its list of skills. It's definitely a grape that rewards patience, holding you in suspense with the promise of getting more and more interesting over time.

Funnily enough, although the varietal is Bordeaux's most important, it never performs alone there. Rather, it's traditionally blended with sibling Merlot and their papa, Cabernet Franc, as well as the occasional Malbec, Petit Verdot and Carmènère. These serve to complement and enhance its intense character. While Cabernet Sauvignon is grown throughout the region, it contributes the most to the distinguished, enchanting wines of the so-called Left Bank (i.e. the reds of the Médoc and Graves; or, more specifically, Margaux, Pessac-Léognan, Saint-Julien and Saint-Estephe, to name a few). In addition to Cab's signature marker of ripe blackcurrant, these tend to display flavours of black cherry, dried herbs, graphite, leather and tobacco.

So great is the reputation of this grape and the wines it produces in Bordeaux, France, that it has inspired a

Key Words
You like a **brawny, complex** red that **doesn't skimp on flavour, body or aromatics**; reds that are obviously dry, but also **smooth textured and rich**; ripe red and black fruit mixed with flavours of mocha, baking, spice, cedar wood and tobacco; a wine that could work as either a drink-right-now option or a 'here's one for your cellar' gift; the **opposite of Pinot Noir**.

You Might Also Like
Priorat, Nero d'Avola, Monastrell, Montepulciano d'Abruzzo, Aglianico, French Malbec, Zinfandel, Portuguese red blends and aged Cabernet Franc from Chinon.

number of copycats around the world. Just consider the celebrated 'Super Tuscans' of central Italy, for example, which see Cabernet Sauvignon and its usual French friends, Merlot and Cab Franc, introduced to local favourite Sangiovese. Although the results are not quite as famous, other notable growing regions to adopt the Cab-led Bordeaux-style blend include South Africa, Australia's Margaret River and Lebanon.

Of course, California, USA, also celebrates Cab in a great many impressive Bordeaux-formula reds, but it's the region's varietal bottlings that have garnered the lion's share of acclaim. It's grown throughout the northern part of the state but, more than anywhere, the grape does its thing the best in Napa – if you can call creating an international cult wine phenomenon a 'thing'. These massive, velvety-textured wines put on more of a razzle-dazzle parade of in-your-face flavours: think juicier, jammier dark fruits, eucalyptus, pepper, baking spices, mocha and cedar wood. While Napa Cab is going to be a consistently expensive category (often exorbitantly so), it is possible to find easier, more reasonably priced examples outside of the prestige region – they're probably going to be less complex, but at the very least, ready to drink young.

Lastly, speaking of good value Cabernet Sauvignon, Chile is great place to look. Vineyards there are planted with cuttings from Bordeaux and tend to produce a friendly, fruit-forward rendition.

Merlot

Say It Right: *Mer-low*

For Merlot, making wine is mostly a family affair. In the Bordeaux region of southwestern France, the grape is famously partnered with its superstar sibling Cabernet Sauvignon and their esteemed parent, Cabernet Franc. In these internationally renowned blends, Merlot's plush texture and forward flavours of baked cherry, cassis and plum are often used to complement Cabernet Sauvignon's comparatively brawnier structure.

But just because Merlot is typically cast as the softer, 'friendlier' brother, doesn't mean it's without the goods to command a lead. While Cabernet Sauvignon sits first chair in the region's so-called 'Left Bank' reds, on the right side of the Gironde estuary, the varietal makes up the majority of the blend in the velvety-rich wines of Pomerol and Saint-Émilion. In these, in addition to its characteristic fruit, Merlot offers complex aromas of mocha, cedar, liquorice, bay leaf and fresh earth.

The most widely planted grape in France, you can also find significant vineyard acreage dedicated to Merlot in Languedoc-Roussillon, although the quality of its work is not as impressive there. Better to focus on the more conversation-worthy Bordeaux-style blends coming out of Friuli in northeastern Italy, and, of course, the 'Super Tuscans' produced on the central eastern coast.

It's actually pretty easy to find Merlot throughout most of Italy (except, perhaps, on the southern end), but beware that a lot of the iterations coming from Lombardy and Alto Adige lose the grape's charming roundness, instead erring on the tart, thin side.

In certain areas of the New World, though, Merlot has flown the coop. In Washington state, Long Island and New York state in the USA, Hawke's Bay in New Zealand and Chile, Merlot is celebrated as a soloist. Washington and Chile in particular have gotten kudos for making a

Notable Regions
France (specifically Bordeaux), California and Washington state in the USA, Spain, Italy, Australia, Chile, New Zealand and Canada.

Drink It With
Grilled, roasted or stewed pork and beef; roast chicken, lamb or duck prepared with a red wine sauce; blue cheese burgers; stewed or roasted root vegetables; French onion soup.

Key Words
You like **medium to full-bodied reds**; want a **dry** wine, but are OK if it drifts over into a realm of more **plush red fruit** flavours; like the notes of **tobacco, dried herbs, cedar wood and bitter chocolate** that oak age can contribute to.

You Might Also Like
Valpolicella Ripasso, Cabernet Sauvignon, Grenache from Spain and Carignan-based red blends.

more polished, Bordeaux-esque style. Northern California is another big name in single varietal Merlots, which are made in a darker, fruitier, more lushly textured style. But it's also used in blends with Cabernet Sauvignon there too, of course - a pattern that is mirrored in Australia and British Columbia, Canada. And in Argentina, it's frequently used in blends with Malbec.

Notable Regions

France (specifically Loire Valley and Bordeaux), Italy (specifically Friuli and Tuscany), California, New York state and Washington state in the USA, Chile, Hungary and Canada.

Drink It With

Grilled and roasted red meat, and also quail and duck; barbecued or wood-fire grilled food; hearty, earthy stews; dishes featuring peppers, aubergine (eggplant) or tomato, and strongly flavoured, tangy goat's cheeses.

Key Words

You like a **dry, medium-bodied, red-fruited wine** with a solid tannic structure and vibrant acidity; **you're on board with charred, smoky mineral tones and a loud green, vegetal profile** (read: the smell of green pepper and jalapeño in your red wine does not freak you out).

You Might Also Like

Carménère, Carignan, Montepulciano and Côtes-du-Rhône/GSM blends.

Cabernet Franc

Say It Right: *Cab-er-nay Fronk*
Other Known Aliases: Bouchet *(Boo-shay)*, Breton *(Bruh-tawn)*

Parents often talk about wanting their children to not only match their successes, but supersede them. So it's probably safe to assume that Cabernet Franc is one hell of a proud papa, because when someone blindly requests a 'glass of Cab', 99% of the time they're expecting its offspring, Cabernet Sauvignon, to appear on the table.

Even in their shared home of Bordeaux, where Cabernet Franc is one of the region's most important and oldest varieties, its major role is as a minor, backseat blending partner to Cabernet Sauvignon in the great reds of the Left Bank. On the right side of the Gironde estuary, in the esteemed sub-regions of Saint-Émilion and Pomerol, it's still not the star of the blend. That honour goes to Merlot, Bordeaux's other big-shot grape (also a Cab Franc progeny). But at least in those wines Cab Franc makes up a more respectable slice of the pie. The varietal is also valued throughout Bordeaux for the fact that it ripens and is picked earlier than Cabernet Sauvignon and Merlot. In challenging vintages when the other two underperform due to weather issues or some other reason, Cab Franc is the reliable, on-hand substitute. Stepping in to support your kids when they come up short? Total Dad move.

But it's not all background chorus gigs for French Cabernet Franc. In the central Loire Valley regions of Chinon, Bourgueil and Saumur-Champigny, it is revered for its work as a single varietal red. And, when left with the spotlight to itself, it is far from shy. Medium-bodied with firm tannins and bright acidity to match, these smooth, elegant wines are known for their loud and unique aromatics. Sure, there's the not-so-unusual collection of red fruit flavours (raspberry is a big one) but, more than anything, these wines are distinctive for

their intense green notes – pepper, green bean, herbs, jalapeño – as well as a smoky, charred rocks mixed with pencil shavings kind of fragrance.

Elsewhere, albeit much less significantly, Cabernet Franc gets to shine on its own in Italy's northeastern region of Friuli; Ontario, Canada, and New York state, Washington state, Michigan and Virginia in the USA. For the most part, though, Cabernet Franc-growing wine regions throughout the world look at the success of its role in Bordeaux blends, and therefore follow that model. Arguably the most notable of these are the 'Super Tuscans' of central Italy, in which it plays a minor role, but California in the USA, Hungary and Australia have also produced some impressive examples.

Pinot Noir

Say It Right: *Pee-no Nwar*
Other Known Aliases: Spätburgunder
(Spate-berg-under), Pinot Nero *(Pee-no Nair-oh)*

Don't let the fact that it is one of the world's most popular and esteemed varietals fool you. Truth be told, Pinot Noir is a little bit of a problem child.

In the vineyard, especially, this ancient grape can be quite prickly and is notorious for putting winemakers through their paces. Put it this way: it has strong feelings about the type of soil it's grown on and is incredibly sensitive to climate, plus, its thin skin makes it an easy target for disease and insects, and it will punish you if you force it to be over productive. And that's not to mention that it can oxidise very quickly during the winemaking process (not a good thing).

From a consumer standpoint, it isn't exactly the easiest or most accessible grape either, especially for those just getting into wine. Aside from having a lighter, more delicate profile (read: more effort to appreciate), all the work and risk on the production side means that the really good, well-made stuff is going to cost you. What's more, about 40 clones of the grape exist, the selection of which can have a huge impact on taste and quality.

But, you know, it's all those challenges and complexities about Pinot Noir's personality that are precisely what make it so irresistible and thrilling. Because despite all that, when it's done right, it rewards you with flavours and textures worthy of effusive rhapsody.

For anyone passionate about Pinot – and there are many – the conversation has to start in Burgundy. So revered is Pinot Noir in its birthplace that, with the exception of Gamay in Beaujolais, it is the region's exclusive red varietal. Burgundy's vineyard landscape is famously complicated and jigsaw puzzle-like, divided between basic village-level sites and the more prestige

Notable Regions
France (specifically Burgundy), California, Oregon and Washington state in the USA, Germany, New Zealand, Australia and Switzerland.

Drink It With
Leaner cuts of beef; braised chicken; roasted duck, lamb or quail; grilled salmon or tuna; practically any dish with mushrooms and root vegetables heavily flavoured with herbs.

Key Words
You like **light-bodied** reds that are dry but **not tannic**; prefer red fruit flavours with tart, **tangy acidity**; are a fan of **herbal and earthy** aromatics; want something complex and don't mind shelling out for it; something **for a special occasion, or to age in your cellar**; the **opposite of Cabernet Sauvignon**.

You Might Also Like
Cru Beaujolais, Zweigelt or St Laurent, Poulsard, Trousseau, Barbera, Frappato and Schiava.

Premier Cru and Grand Cru areas. Although this gives wine drinkers more homework, it's an ideal setup for Pinot Noir, a master at conveying sense of place. While this kind of transparency produces wine that will vary from one vineyard site to another, generally speaking, you can expect red Burgundy to be light-bodied and ethereal, with soft tannins and tart, tangy notes of sour cherry and cranberry. These wines display a strong earthy vibe as well – think foraging for mushrooms and herbs in the forest. And with age, these wines can take on flavours of wild game.

Pinot Noir's influence in France extends beyond Burgundy: it's one of three varietals allowed in the production of Champagne, it's responsible for the slightly rare and mineral-toned reds and rosés of Sancerre and it produces some very unique examples in Alsace and the Jura. Otherwise, you can find some very good versions in parts of northern Italy and Switzerland, as well as Germany, where it tends to exhibit more fruit and power.

Picky Pinot has also successfully settled in several of the New World's big-name winegrowing hubs: California and Washington state in the USA, Chile, south Australia and Central Otago in New Zealand. There, the grape goes more the way of baked raspberry and plum and takes on a riper, arguably more friendly personality. While still technically a light-bodied grape, its texture tends to be on the plush side, and its aromatics drift into a realm of 'prettier' flavours like baking spices, tea and tobacco leaves, and dark flowers. Oregon, USA, its other notable New World home, should not be overlooked, and is better known for producing Pinot in a more restrained, Burgundian style.

Syrah

Notable Regions
France (especially the Rhône Valley), Australia, Spain, northern California and Washington state in the USA, Argentina, Chile and Italy.

Drink It With
Meat-based dishes with smoke and spice: barbecue, bacon cheeseburgers, carnitas tacos; meaty red-sauce pastas, and mushrooms.

Key Words
Old World-style: you like **medium to full-bodied dry reds**, with red fruit and **savoury flavours**; like bacon so much you want to smell it in wine. New World-style: like a full-bodied dry, but **fruit-forwards red wine with a lush texture** and smooth tannins; **prefer ripe black fruit flavours**.

You Might Also Like
For Old-World, try Blaüfrankish, Nero d'Avola, Barolo and Mourvedre. For New World, try Petit Verdot, Malbec, Pinotage, Touriga Nacional/Portuguese red blends and Aglianico.

Say It Right: *Sir-ah*
Other Known Aliases: Shiraz *(Sher-az)*

Grapes, like people, often take on very different personalities depending on their environment. To the point where meeting an Australian Shiraz after years of being friends with French Syrah might feel like a bit of a duplicitous encounter. Technically it's the same coin, but its two sides are totally unique (and, in this case, both famous in their own right).

On one end you have the primal, savage Syrahs of France's Rhône Valley. There, the grape produces bold wines with unmistakable flavours of cured meat, bacon fat, wild berries and bramble, leather, black olive, pepper, smoke, tar, tobacco and lavender. Think of it as the Ernest Hemingway of reds: all broody and irreverent with an unapologetic manly-man charm, but also sophisticated, incisive and strangely poetic. It is the exclusive red varietal of the northern part of the region, responsible for the celebrated – and, in some cases, legendary – reds of Cornas, Côte-Rôtie, Hermitage, Crozes-Hermitage and Saint-Joseph. In the southern part of the Rhône it moves into more of a supportive role, adding texture and its distinctive feral edge to the Grenache-dominated red blends of Châteauneuf-du-Pape, Gigondas, Vacqueyras, Rasteau and Côtes-du-Rhône.

On the flip side of the coin (and hemisphere), you have Shiraz, the grape's Australian alter ego. As the most widely produced variety in the country, it's a total icon; a big, if not the only, reason for Australia's status as a major player on the wine world stage. In this home, however, it shows a completely different side of its personality: less rough-edged, savoury, wild animal, and more full-bodied cornucopia of lush, ripe, black fruits (plums! blueberries! blackberries! black cherry and raspberry!), mixed with intoxicating flavours of mocha, baking spices, pepper, pipe tobacco and eucalyptus.

A Quick Word about 'Junior': Petite Sirah

If you're into Californian wine then you might have also heard of Petite Sirah, Syrah's offspring with an almost unheard-of French grape called Peloursin. The grape is best known for its role in the wines of northern and central California, where it is either used to add weight and texture to red blends (usually starring Cabernet Sauvignon or Zinfandel), or as a single varietal. When flying solo, Petit Sirah tends to make full-throttle, big-boned tannic reds brimming with rich, dark fruit, tobacco and baking spices, dried herbs, and a distinct meatiness (just like Syrah). Go classic and enjoy it alongside some simple barbecued meat and vegetables.

The most famous expressions of this style of Shiraz come from the Barossa Valley in South Australia, though it's worth noting that cooler-climate regions can actually produce spicier, earthier renditions more akin to those of the Rhône. And, as in France, it is also a popular choice in blends, frequently partnered with Grenache or Cabernet Sauvignon to make powerful, opulent reds.

Outside of these two signature growing regions, production of Syrah has been on the rise in central Spain and Chile, as well as been successful in the hands of some Rhône-inspired producers in northern California and Washington state in the USA.

Grenache

Say It Right: *Gruh-nah-sh*
Other Known Aliases: Garnacha *(Gar-nat-chah)*,
Cannonau *(Canon-ow)*

One of the most widely planted grapes in the world,
think of Grenache as the friendlier, sweeter 'nice guy'
member in a gang of mostly rugged, brawny characters.
With its characteristic ripe, concentrated red fruit
flavours, moderate tannins and plush texture,
herb-and-spice-scented Grenache is particularly
valued for its ability to round out the rougher edges
of its frequent blending partners.

You can find the grape throughout southern France,
where it is typically buddied-up with meatier, bolder,
more structured varietals like Syrah, Mourvèdre,
Carignan and, occasionally, Cinsault. Grenache's
partnership with Syrah and Mourvedre is so well
established, in fact, that the trio are commonly
identified under a singular acronym: 'GSM.' The reds of
Côtes-du-Rhône, Côtes-du-Rhône Villages, Gigondas and
Vacqueyras in southern Rhône and Faugères, Minervois,
Corbières and Fitou in the Languedoc-Roussillon can all
be credited as the work of Grenache and its cronies. And
let's not forget to also give a shout-out to the crew for
their hand in the dry rosés of the area, from places such
as Tavel and Lirac.

In most of these, Grenache makes up the bulk of
the blend but, without question, its most important
leadership role is in the world-famous reds of southern
Rhône's Châteauneuf-du-Pape region. These heady,
opulent wines can be made from a combination of 13
select grapes, but it is Grenache, often acting as the
dominant player, that gives Châteauneuf its signature
note of luscious fruit jam.

Notable Regions
France (specifically
southern Rhône and
Languedoc-Roussillon),
Spain, Australia, Italy
(specifically, Sardinia)
and California in
the USA.

Drink It With
Well-spiced meats using
grilled, barbecue, and
braised preparations;
dishes seasoned with
Moroccan and Middle
Eastern spice blends, for
example, lamb tagine.

Key Words
You like a red that
is **fruit-driven**, with
concentrated, **slightly
cooked flavours of red
and black fruit**; reds
that feel like they've
been seasoned with a
bit of **pepper and spice**;
not crazy about crunchy
tannins, favouring
instead something with
plush texture that's a
little plump and boozy.

You Might Also Like
Valpolicella Ripasso,
Zinfandel, American
Merlot, Nerello
Mascalese, Australian
Shiraz and
Argentinian Malbec.

Now, Châteauneuf reds are technically dry (albeit rich and fruit-forward), but elsewhere in the southwest of France, Grenache's natural fruity sweetness is cranked up and put on display in the *vin doux naturel* dessert wines of Banyuls, Rasteau and Maury.

Garnacha plays an equally important role in its native Spain, where it contributes to the country's best red wines. It is both the power player in the big, sultry red blends of Priorat, and an important, edge-softening assistant to Tempranillo in Rioja. You're most likely to see the grape throughout the northern half of the country, making round, spicy, fruit-driven reds, as well as some vibrant, juicy dry rosés.

Grenache can also be found on the Italian island of Sardinia masquerading under the name Cannonau. There, it is produced as a single-varietal wine known for its boozy heft and aromas of dried herbs, red fruit and spice. Otherwise, look out for GSM blends from central and southern California and Washington state in the USA and southern Australia.

Say It Right: *Bar-bare-ah*

Notable Regions
Italy (specifically, Piedmont and Emilia-Romagna), California in the USA, Argentina and South Africa.

Drink It With
Red-sauce pastas and pizzas; grilled pork; burgers; roasted vegetables (especially mushrooms and peppers) and charcuterie and robust hard cheeses such as Pecorino.

Key Words
You like **lighter to medium-bodied red** wines and *a lot* of **tangy acidity**; are not looking for anything too tannic; gravitate towards riper-tasting **red and black fruit flavours** and are into the smell of **herbs and spice**; want something that is **easy-drinking** and not going to deplete your funds.

You Might Also Like
Nerello Mascalese, Mencia, Valpolicella blend, Dolcetto, Cinsault and Zweigelt.

In any story there's the star, and then there's the supporting character – that friendly, reliable, good-but-not-quite-as-great sidekick who lives in the shadow of the lead. That's essentially the relationship between Nebbiolo and Barbera, the key red grape players in northwestern Italy's famed Piedmont region.

While Barbera is the region's most widely planted grape, Nebbiolo occupies its best, most important vineyards in the legendary sites of Barolo and Barbaresco. Where Nebbiolo is fiercely tannic, generally requiring long aging to reveal the great depth and complexity of its flavour profile, medium-bodied Barbera offers a softer texture with low tannins and bright acidity, easy and ready to drink upon release. Top Nebbiolo bottles live in the 'save it for a special occasion' price range, but Barberas remain consistently in the easy and accessible weeknight staple realm. You get the idea. But please don't read the comparison between Nebbiolo and Barbera as a slight against the latter. Barbera is a populist wine, rustic and charming, with notes of mulberry, sour cherry and plum, combined with dried wild herbs, liquorice and spice. Its wines offer an enviable balance of bold, concentrated flavour with a punchy, juicy acidity that allows it to still taste light on its feet. It's what makes it such a great match for rich, fattier food, as well as savoury dishes that benefit from a fruit counterpoint.

The grape's most pedigreed expressions come from Piedmont's Asti and Alba sub-regions, and it's well worth the extra money to see what happens when this 'stepsister' grape is taken more seriously. Otherwise, if you're looking to see a different side of Barbera, check out New World versions from Argentina and California, USA, where the wine takes on a riper, more fruit-forward character – think blackberry-cherry jam scented with vanilla and purple flowers.

Gamay

Say It Right: *Gah-may*

Notable Regions
France (specifically,
Beaujolais and the Loire
Valley), Switzerland,
northern California and
Oregon in the USA,
Canada and
New Zealand.

Drink It With
Picnic-friendly foods:
cheese and charcuterie,
savoury quiches, light
salads; burgers; seared
tuna or salmon steak;
roast duck, veal, quail
and chicken; autumn
(fall) vegetables or,
honestly, nothing at all.

Key Words
You enjoy a **light-
bodied, lower-tannin,
high-acid red** with fresh
fruit flavours; like a red
that benefits from a
slight chill and is **ready
to drink** as soon as you
get it home; want to
seek out wines with the
potential to **over-deliver
for the price**.

You Might Also Like
Pinot Noir, Frappato,
Zweigelt, Saint Laurent,
Cinsault, Langhe Rosso,
Valdigué, Trousseau
and Poulsard.

It's been quite the rollercoaster ride for Gamay and its iconic growing region, Beaujolais. The story is not unlike that of the small-town band that skyrockets to mass-market success thanks to a major pop hit. After a reputation-defining run in the limelight, there's the inevitable fall from grace thanks in no small part to questionable quality and oversaturation of the market. Their fame-making tune becomes a cliché, and it's not until the band returns to its roots and refocuses on what they do best that they are once again championed and turn into a cult-favourite comeback.

The southeastern French region has been making a name for itself with Gamay since at least the 1500s. Beaujolais' signature fresh-fruited light red, made from 100% of the varietal, had been happily living life as the swiggable (not an insult), affordable alternative to the high-brow Pinot Noirs of its neighbour to the north, the Côte d'Or of Burgundy. Then, in the 1970s and 1980s, Beaujolais Nouveau became a thing – a big thing. What originated as an unassuming practice of releasing some of the month-old, just-finished-fermenting 'nouveau' wine from that year's harvest snowballed into an international extravaganza (well played, marketing). Seeing money signs, much of the region abandoned tradition and quality and succumbed to mass-production, pumping out the boozy, tropical fruit punch of a wine that had become the Nouveau movement brand.

And look, it's not like it isn't fun to dip into some punch every once in a while at a party, but the problem is that when something becomes synonymous with novelty, no one really takes it seriously or expects much out it. And so it was with Beaujolais' reputation for quite some time. Eventually, though, as the Nouveau shine wore off, the spotlight was able to shift onto the small group of dedicated producers who had weathered the storm and

The New Nouveau

Because everything old is new again, it shouldn't come as a surprise that some producers are reviving the Nouveau tradition, making it cool again for a generation of ever more discerning wine drinkers. While you can find releases from a handful of benchmark Beaujolais producers (Marcel Lapierre, Jean Foillard, PUR) looking to flip the page on that dark spot in their region's history, the concept has really taken off with a number of winemakers in California, Oregon and the Finger Lakes in New York state, USA. There, a confident 'See, Nouveau doesn't have to suck' attitude has produced a crop of diverse wines that celebrate the fun, frivolous nature of the style without compromising quality. Beyond the traditional Gamay, the line up of American Nouveaus includes Pinot Noir, Pinot Gris, Chardonnay, Merlot, Chenin Blanc and Valdigué, to name a few.

stayed true to the original course. These winemakers, mostly working off the top, 'cru'-level sub-regions – of which there are ten – proved that Beaujolais can produce wines with elegance, complexity and even the ability to age. The wines from these quality-designated crus, which also happen to be a basecamp of the French natural wine movement, are the current sommelier and wine nerd equivalent of catnip. Their charming, tart berries and cherries-meets-herbs-meets-purple flowers-meets-spice-meets-black tea-meets-fresh earth experience is not only incredibly food-friendly, but also has the added bonus of still being a relatively good deal.

Gamay does have a life outside of Beaujolais, by the way. In France, it is also at home in the Anjou and Touraine regions of the Loire Valley, where it produces easy-drinking, juicy light reds and fruity rosés. While across the pond in the USA, a number of fresh-faced producers in Northern California, Oregon and the Finger Lakes in upstate New York have been producing fun, slightly riper and often quirky renditions of the grape.

The Crus of Beaujolais

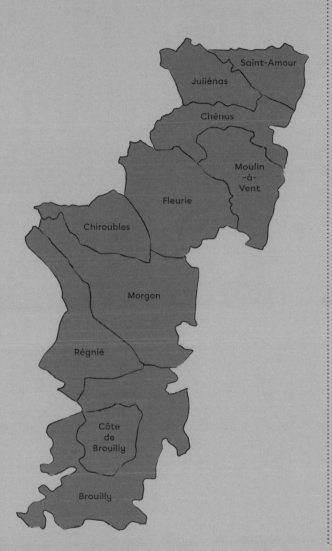

Saint-Amour

Juliénas

Chénas

Moulin -à- Vent

Fleurie

Chiroubles

Morgon

Régnié

Côte de Brouilly

Brouilly

Getting to Know the Cru

Getting serious about drinking Gamay means getting to know the crus of Beaujolais, aka the ten designated quality growing areas where the grape achieves rockstar status. Representing only 15% of production in the region – more than half is still dedicated to basic Beaujolais and Nouveau, and only about a quarter to the next level up, Villages – these are the names you're going to want to look out for on labels and wine lists. From there, it's just a matter of digging in to the fun homework (aka drinking) to discover if you're more a fan of the bolder, fuller (relatively speaking) expressions from Moulin-à-Vent, Morgon and Régnié, or, if you prefer the more delicate, floral touches of Fleurie and Chénas.

Carignan

Say It Right: *Care-een-yawn*
Other Known Aliases: Cariñena *(Car-een-yen-ah)*,
Carignano *(Car-een-yan-no)*, Mazuelo *(Maz-way-low)*

Notable Regions
Southwestern France,
Spain, Algeria, Tunisia,
Chile and California in
the USA.

Drink It With
Hearty stews and
roasted red meat dishes
with a heavy baking
spices influence, cured
meats and game birds.

Key Words
You like **rustic,
full-bodied red wines**
with **bold acidity and
tannins**; gravitate
towards **red and black
fruit flavours** and
**appreciate a wine that
smells like cured meat**
and baking spices; **don't
want to break the bank.**

You Might Also Like
Northern Rhône Syrahs,
Zinfandel and Aglianico.

Carignan may have once been the most widely planted red varietal in France, but that does not mean it's ever been among the most popular, or important. Quite the opposite, in fact. The casual wine drinker has probably never even heard of it, thanks to a legacy of being used in the simple, unmarked table wines of southwestern France and its native northern Spain. It's what you might call a 'workhorse' grape; a likeable-but-not-outstanding Average Joe type that keeps its nose to the grind, works hard and produces well without having an ego.

Because it's a high-yielding grape, it's long been an attractive candidate for overproduction and overextension in the 'quantity over quality' game. And, as a result, its potential and charms went largely overlooked. Admittedly, it's not exactly a diamond-in-the-rough kind of grape; it's a genuinely rustic and gruff varietal, producing dark-fruited, meaty, robust wines marked by high acidity and alcohol, and intense tannins. But now that it's being taken more seriously, especially when old-vine grapes are being used, Carignan is proving to be a valued contributor in the well-made, value-driven blends of Corbières, Fitou and Minervois in France's Languedoc-Roussillon region, as well as a co-conspirator in the dry blended rosés of Provençe.

Back in its Spanish homeland, Cariñena, or Mazuelo, as it's known, remains an important partner to Grenache in the ripe-smoky-herbal red wines of Priorat, as well as a valued supporting character to Tempranillo in some of the revered reds of Rioja. Meanwhile in northern California, USA, it's experiencing a mini-resurgence in both blended and single varietal wines.

Malbec

Notable Regions
Argentina, southwestern France, Chile, California in the USA, south Australia and South Africa.

Drink It With
Meat, meat and more meat (sorry, vegetarians!); grilled steak and smoked lamb work especially well (as do burger versions of either); cassoulet; farro with stewed root vegetables, and mushrooms.

Key Words
You definitely like **medium to full-bodied reds** with **loads of black fruit** flavours; enjoy something **lush and smooth**, not too tannic; are looking for a **friendly, good-value** option that **doesn't necessarily need food**.

You Might Also Like
Merlot, Zinfandel, Mourvèdre, Shiraz from Australia, California Cabernet Sauvignon and Touriga Nacional-based blends from Portugal.

You probably don't realise it, but Malbec's story is actually a bit of a rags-to-riches tale. It's difficult to imagine in today's reality, where mention of the grape instantly conjures images of the plush, dark-fruited red that has become the unofficial mascot of Argentina's wine industry. But the truth of the matter is, for all its current popularity and shiny stardom, Malbec comes from pretty average, humble origins.

In its native southwest France, the grape otherwise known as Côt produces medium-bodied, rustic, brambly reds with a more pronounced earthy, tannic edge than its southern hemisphere counterpart. The most renowned of this rough-and-tumble, gritty style comes from the region of Cahors, and, for what it's worth, these wines are just about the best thing you could ever drink alongside a big plate of duck cassoulet. Malbec has also historically been a significant grape in nearby Bordeaux, where it has traditionally played sidekick to Cabernet Sauvignon, as well as in the Loire, where it adds dark fruit flavour and boozy oomph to Gamay and Cabernet Franc-based blends.

But it wasn't until a Frenchman brought the varietal to Argentina in the mid-to-late 19th century that Malbec got its big break. In its adopted home, where it is now the second most-planted variety (but definitely the most important), Malbec shows off a softer, more vampy side of its personality. With moderate acidity and just enough tannic structure to keep the whole thing technically dry, these wines swaddle your tongue in a velvet-smooth blanket of ripe dark fruit (blackberry, blueberry and plum), spice and violets.

You can find the grape being cultivated across the country, but the high-altitude vineyards of Mendoza, Argentina, are where it does its best-known work.

For the most part, these generously flavoured, value-friendly wines are designed for right-now drinking, but if you want to see how the grape evolves with the influence of extended oak aging, look for a higher-end 'Reserva' bottle.

Besides France and Argentina, you can find Malbec in places like California in the USA, South Australia and Chile, where it is typically teamed up with its old pal from Bordeaux, Cabernet Sauvignon.

Zinfandel

Say It Right: *Zin-fan-del*
Other Known Aliases: Primitivo *(Pree-mee-tee-vo)*,
Tribidrag *(Tri-bidd-rag)*

Zinfandel may not get the international attention and acclaim that the USA's Pinot Noirs, Cabernet Sauvignons and Chardonnays do, but it is nevertheless an – if not the iconic 'American' wine. As American as apple pie, you might say. Except, of course, it technically isn't.

Though it was long thought to be and promoted as an indigenous varietal to the United States, the grape is actually native to Croatia, where it was originally known as Tribidrag. It didn't land state-side until sometime in the early 19th century, eventually making California its home in the 1850s. The trajectory feels a little like that of the kid who didn't get much attention in its hometown, but then, given the opportunity to start fresh at a new school in a new town, took on a different identity and flourished. Zinfandel was so popular in California, in fact, that up until 1998, it was the most widely planted red grape in the state (currently it's number two, with Cabernet Sauvignon in the lead).

Granted, a big chunk of the grape's production is dedicated to making the maligned semi-sweet, actually-pink-not-white wine known as 'white Zinfandel'. While this may be some of Zinfandel's most recognisable work in California, it is by no means its best. Grown throughout the state, 'Zin' is at the top of its game in Sonoma, Napa, the Sierra Foothills and Lodi in the north, as well as Paso Robles in the centre.

Typically, these medium to full-bodied wines are robust and high-octane (aka boozy), delivering a wallop of berry fruit flavours so ripe it borders on jammy and raisinated. Notes of baking spices, sage, pepper, smoked meat and tobacco are also common markers.

Notable Regions
California in the USA, Italy (specifically Puglia), Croatia.

Drink It With
Barbecued meats glazed in a sweeter-style sauce; lamb or steak; chilli con carne; spicy Mexican food such as carnitas tacos and chicken mole; burgers; sausage and pepper sandwiches or pizza.

Key Words
You like **medium to full-bodied** reds with moderate tannins; big, **juicy, ripe red-berry flavours** are your friend; love the idea of something that smells **smoky and a little meaty**; want to pick a wine that's **smooth but packs a punch**.

You Might Also Like
Grenache, Carignan, Syrah, American Merlot, Nero d'Avola and Malbec.

It's worth mentioning, too, that Zinfandel's long history in California makes it possible to find some exceptional, ageworthy old-vine expressions of the grape.

Although producers in parts of Australia, South Africa, South America and Croatia (of course) have had some success with Zinfandel, the varietal's only other real home of note is in Puglia, otherwise known as the heel to Italy's boot. There, it goes by yet another name – Primitivo – and is used to produce similarly rich, dark fruit-driven single varietal reds, or to add body and concentrated fruit flavour to blends with the native, highly tannic Negroamaro.

Notable Regions
Bordeaux and southwestern France, Spain, Australia, Chile, California in the USA and South Africa.

Drink It With
Anything you would have with a Cabernet Sauvignon-based blend from Bordeaux. A nice cut of steak; a rich red-sauce and meat-based stew and heartier grains and legumes. Non-creamy dishes with mushrooms and other earthy ingredients also work well.

Key Words
You want a full-bodied, **rich, dark-fruited red** with **grippy tannins**; are a fan of **fuller-bodied red blends**; want something that's going to be a **bang for your buck**.

You Might Also Like
Shiraz, Mourvèdre, a Bordeaux-style blend, Nero d'Avola, Petit Sirah and Touriga Nacional.

Petit Verdot

Say It Right: *Puh-tee Ver-doh*

Tasting a well made, blended wine is like hearing a choir singing in harmony. Within the group you have your strong, powerful, leadership voices, but also an assembly of 'smaller' voices filling in the gaps. While perhaps a less glamorous role, it is nevertheless an incredibly important one. A fact Petit Verdot knows all too well.

Full-bodied and fiercely tannic, this boozy, high-acid red is bursting with flavours of ripe black fruits, smoke and spice, as well as wild herbs and flowers. It's a whole lot of wine on its own, so even in small doses it makes a big impact on a blend. In the iconic red blends from Bordeaux's Left Bank, it's used sparingly but effectively – usually no more than two to three percent of the entire blend – to help punch up the colour, tannic structure and floral-herbal aromatics of the final wine. Its calling card reads pretty much the same in its other important growing regions of central Spain, Chile, California in the USA and South Africa.

That being said, Petit Verdot has a decent-sized fanbase in parts of Australia, where, in addition to vamping up Bordeaux-style blends, it is also appreciated as a single varietal.

Mourvèdre

Say It Right: *Moo-ved-druh*
Other Known Aliases: Monastrell *(Mon-ah-strell)*,
Mataro *(Mah-tar-oh)*

Notable Regions
Spain, France
(specifically the Rhône
Valley and Languedoc-
Roussillon), Australia,
California in the USA
and South Africa.

Drink It With
Grilled or roasted meat
(beef, pork sausage,
game birds); charcuterie;
and vegetables seasoned
with woody herbs such as
rosemary and thyme.

Key Words
You're into **full-throttle
reds** – **chunky tannins**,
lots of body and **weight**,
high-alcohol, powerful
flavours of **black fruit,
earth and herbs**, and
a generous amount of
acidity to back it all up;
want something
with a **broody,
brawny** personality.

You Might Also Like
Cabernet Sauvignon,
Syrah, Petit Sirah,
Malbec, Touriga
Nacional-based blends
from Portugal and
Petit Verdot.

Mourvèdre is kind of like that member of the band that you always name last, almost as an aside, after the other, 'more famous' ones have been listed.

The 'M' in GSM – the shorthand for the trio behind the majority of reds in southern Rhône and the Languedoc-Roussillon in France – Mourvèdre definitely takes a backseat to its partners Grenache and Syrah. But just because the grape is a little less popular and well-known, doesn't mean its contributions to the mix are any less valuable. Known for producing hearty, tannic wines so thick you can practically sink your teeth into them (not literally, but you get the idea), Mourvèdre is the essential component that adds structure and body to the blend.

And aside from its muscle, the varietal also offers flavours of ripe blackberries, a bite of black pepper and spice, as well as a mildly savage, meaty-gamey quality. The intensity of its personality means that it rarely performs solo. The closest Mourvèdre really comes to taking centre stage is in the powerful reds and rosés of Bandol, in Provence, where it must make up at least half of the blend. And, no joke, these wines are brawny, almost an antithesis to the breezy, idyllic landscape where they're grown. The reds are so tannic in their youth that they ought not be served without the offer, 'Would you like a side of meat with that?,' and the rosés have enough character to shut down the rumour that the category is merely frivolous summertime swill.

In its native Spain, Monastrell, as it's known, makes equally big, broad, fruit-driven reds, albeit with slightly softer curved edges. Most of its production is concentrated in the centre and southeastern parts of the country, where it is used to make single varietal

wines as well as the expected red blend, most of which fall in the friendly and affordable price range. And, further to the northeast in Penedes, it's even being used in the production of rosé Cava.

In California, USA, and Australia, Mourvèdre has been long masquerading as Mataro – so well, in fact, that it wasn't until recently that people even realised the two are actually one and the same. In both places, it's rustic, gnarly and typically used in southern Rhône-style blends, although you can find some very well made old-vine varietal expressions (read: pricey) from California.

Nebbiolo

Say It Right: *Neb-ee-yolo*
Other Known Aliases: Spanna *(Spah-nah)*,
Chiavennasca *(Ki-ah-vay-nah-sah)*

There are those who are bright, easy and cheerful; excited and ready to welcome you with open arms from the get-go. And then there are those who are more guarded and reserved – temperamental even – who require time to open up and reveal the complexities of their personality. Nebbiolo is very much the latter.

One of Italy's most important red varietals, responsible for the prestigious, enthralling reds of Barolo and Barbaresco, Nebbiolo is a star and it knows it. Starting in the vineyard, it's extremely picky about where it grows and the type of soil it's planted on, favouring, almost exclusively, the fog-covered hills of the small Piedmont sub-regions (in fact, *nebbia* is Italian for 'fog', so you can take a wild guess as to where the inspiration for the grape's name came from). It also flowers early, takes forever to ripen, and is highly susceptible to a number of diseases – all potential red flags that require a great deal of skill to manage. And on top of all that, Nebbiolo is naturally high in tannin, resulting in wines that typically benefit from long aging before being released, and even then, are often at their best after spending several more years (if not decades) in the bottle. Warning: impatient wine drinkers best not apply. Not to mention the fact that the amount of work and time that goes into making Nebbiolo's greatest hits – Barolo and Barbaresco – keeps them pretty firmly in the 'not cheap' price bracket.

Like a true diva, Nebbiolo does not make shy wines. Despite its lighter colour, the varietal famously produces full-throttle reds that are loaded with tannin, acidity and alcohol. The best among them will shout a seduction of aromatics at you from the glass. Dried rose petals, cherry, cranberry, tar, liquorice and anise are all common markers, but as the wine ages you can also expect to

Notable Regions
Northwestern Italy (specifically Piedmont and Lombardy), California in the USA, Switzerland, Australia and Argentina.

Drink It With
Steak with herbs and butter; coq au vin; tea-smoked duck; osso bucco; mushroom-based sauces and dishes (e.g. mushroom risotto) and, if you're fancy, anything with black truffle shaved over it.

Key Words
You are **not scared of tannins**; like **complex**, medium-bodied reds with a **super earthy and savoury** flavour profile; are interested in trying something with a bit of age on it, or **ages well**, and don't mind that that means it's going to be more **expensive**.

You Might Also Like
Dolcetto, Negroamaro, Brunello di Montalcino, Aglianico, aged Rioja and Bandol.

find intriguing savoury notes of balsamic, tobacco leaf, leather, cured meat and smoke. Speaking in broad terms, Barolo is going to make a broodier, brawnier expression of Nebbiolo, while Barbarescos are (relatively) softer and more elegant. And so, as with a diva, you forgive them all the pre-performance attitude, antics and demands because, in the end, they have the goods to back it all up. While perhaps not the easiest to like, these wines are definitely hard not to love.

Elsewhere in Piedmont, you can find some more accessible renditions of Nebbiolo from places such as Ghemme, Gattinara, Carema and Roero, as well as the general Langhe region (which are the friendliest and easiest to drink upon release of the bunch). Some very good versions are also made in Valtellina, in the neighbouring Lombardy region. Outside of northwestern Italy, plantings of the grape are surprisingly scarce given its worldwide fame, although a handful of producers in Switzerland, California, USA and Australia have done well with it.

Tempranillo

Notable Regions
Spain, Portugal, Argentina, New Zealand, California in the USA, France and Australia.

Drink It With
Grilled, roasted and smoked preparations of meat and vegetables; red sauce pasta dishes; chilli and other meaty stews seasoned with warming spices; Mexican food.

Key Words
You like a wine that is dry and **medium to full-bodied** with **solid acidity and tannins**; go for something a little more rustic/musky and savoury; want a wine that **ages well**; enjoy the smell of coconut and dill caused by new American oak.

You Might Also Like
Aged Barolo or Barbaresco, Agiorgitiko, Zinfandel, Brunello di Montalcino, Right Bank Bordeaux and Montepulciano.

Say It Right: *Temp-rah-nee-yo*
Other Known Aliases: Tinto Fino *(Teen-toe Feen-oh)*, Cencibel *(Sen-si-belle)*, Tinta Roriz *(Teen-ta Roar-eez)*

In the world of Spanish wine, Tempranillo is treated like the beloved first-born child: it gets all the praise, most of the attention and is a huge source of pride. As the country's leading red grape, it is best known for being the driving force behind the legendary reds of Rioja and Ribera del Duero.

Although the grape is grown throughout the country, it does its most significant, cherished work in the north-central Rioja region. There, it is partnered with Garnacha, Mazuelo (aka Carignan) and the local Graciano, to make bold, characterful wines capable of long aging. You might say that in the blend, Tempranillo is what gives the wine its guts. The full-bodied varietal gets high marks for tannin, acidity and alcohol, and its wines are known for displaying flavours ranging from strawberry and dried fruits to savoury herbs, leather, spice and tobacco.

Within the region, the style of the wine can vary significantly based on the philosophy of the winemaker and how long it's aged. Traditionalists tend to go for a more broody, earthy style and prefer aging in American oak, which lends signature notes of coconut, dill, baking spices and vanilla. More 'modern' producers will age the wine in small French barrels called *barriques* to produce a flashier version that focuses more on ripe fruit and oak. In terms of aging, look for the words *'joven'* or *'crianza'* for young, less-aged expressions, and 'reserva' and 'gran reserva' for those that have spent significantly more time hanging out in barrel and bottle before release. FYI, the aging terminology applies across other regions and red grape varietals in Spain, so it's a good list to commit to memory.

Tempranillo's other big feature role in is the reds of the Ribera del Duero in the centre of the country. Under the alias Tinto Fino, it's famous for producing rich, complex single varietal wines of the smoky tobacco-coffee and cocoa-concentrated fruit persuasion. Not to mention the influential producer Vega Sicilia has made a name for itself by using the grape alongside Cabernet Sauvignon, Merlot and Malbec to create a Bordeaux-inspired blend.

Outside of Spain, Tempranillo doesn't make much news. Aside from being an important grape in the blend used to make Port, Portugal's legendary dessert wine, Tempranillo only really shows up in small amounts from places like Argentina, New Zealand and California in the USA.

Sangiovese

Say It Right: *San-geo-vay-zay*

When it comes to Italy, there are a lot of grapes to talk about – 350 if you just count those that have been recognised as 'official' – but only a handful that you can't not talk about. As a case in point, there's no skipping over Sangiovese: the high-to-low charmer of central Italy that also happens to be the country's most widely planted varietal.

The ironic thing about Sangiovese, of course, is that for a grape that is so well-known and internationally recognised, its personality is not always so simple to pinpoint. It can just as easily be the stuff of uncomplicated table wines (à la bulbous-bottle-wrapped-in-a-straw-basket style), or make some of the most enthralling, complex and highly regarded reds in the world. Part of this inconsistency has to do with the fact that this old variety has, over many years, spawned several clones, and not all of them are capable of achieving the same quality. The other key element of the equation is vineyard site, which can dramatically alter the ultimate character of the wine produced.

In terms of being able to experience the full range of Sangiovese's repertoire, Tuscany is where it's at. In Chianti, where the grape accounts for the overwhelming majority of the blend, you can find everything from basic, fresh red-fruited versions to the higher-quality 'Classico' designations (think flavours of roasted tomato, balsamic vinegar and herbs), as well as the more intense and savoury-toned 'Riserva' expressions that have seen a couple years of aging. Medium-bodied and acid-flush Sangiovese also produces some of its highest calibre work as Brunello di Montalcino. These more firmly structured, aged Sangioveses take on darker fruit flavours, as well as notes of baking spices, leather, tobacco and dried flowers and herbs. For a lighter, kind of gateway version of these (in both price-point and flavour), look

Notable Regions
Italy (specifically Tuscany), Argentina, France, California in the USA and Australia.

Drink It With
Pretty much all things tomato and tomato sauce-based, and generally any flavours and ingredients that are staples in Mediterranean cuisine; salami, grilled steak, and braised chicken; ratatouille; mushroom-based dishes and sauces.

Key Words
You like a wine that's **medium-bodied** with **bright red fruit** flavours and a **decent tannins**; find the idea of something **rustic and savoury** appealing, and you're very fond of **herbal** aromas and the taste of **olive brine**; want something to drink on pizza night.

You Might Also Like
Young, crianza-level Tempranillo, Barbaresco or Nebbiolo from Valtellina, Mencia, Barbera, Valpolicella and Cru Beaujolais.

for bottles from Rosso di Montalcino. Nearby, too, Sangiovese dominates the wines of the tasty though decidedly less acclaimed Vino Nobile di Montepulciano and its younger sibling version, Rosso di Montepulciano (neither of which, FYI, have any relation to the grape Montepulciano – confusing, I know).

And, of course, we would be remiss not to give a shout-out to Sangiovese's role in another one of the region's highly publicised wines, the so-called 'Super Tuscans'. These big, bold, Bordeaux-by-way-of-Tuscany reds see the grape teamed up with some unexpected partners such as Cabernet Sauvignon, Cabernet Franc and Merlot, and are aged in small French oak barrels.

Beyond Tuscany, Sangiovese's influence extends east through Umbria and the Marche, as well as north in Emilia-Romagna. Outside of Italy, however, Sangiovese doesn't have much reach, with some examples to be found in California in the USA, Argentina, Australia and the French island of Corsica, where it actually gets some decent play.

Notable Regions
South Africa.

Drink It With
Meat, and lots of it.
But if you want to get
specific, barbecued food
works especially well.

Key Words
You want something
**dark, full-bodied and
boldly tannic**; might
say that you like
rough-edged, muscular,
and just a little bit
aggressive wines –
nothing shy or delicate;
your thing is **earthy and
smoky flavours.**

You Might Also Like
Syrah, Petit Sirah,
Negroamaro, Petit
Verdot and Mourvèdre.

Pinotage

Say It Right: *Pee-no-taj*

Usually when you meet someone's parents it just clicks: 'Ohhhhh, that's why you're like that, that explains it.' Occasionally, however, there's a total disconnect: 'Whoa, where did you come from?' It's a reaction that Pinotage has probably grown quite accustomed to by now.

South Africa's signature grape first was conceived in 1925 by viticultural scientist Abraham Perold. His hope was that by crossing Pinot Noir with Cinsault, you'd end up with a grape that had the aromatic and flavour complexity of the former, combined with the latter's sturdy productivity in the vineyard. In the end, Pinotage had its own idea about the kind of grape it was, and the wine it would grow up to make.

Unlike the delicate, light-bodied wines produced by Pinot Noir, dark, thick-skinned Pinotage makes a hardy, boozy red with fierce tannins. It doesn't share Pinot's naturally high acidity either, so the rich flavour of ripe black fruits is even more pronounced. Notes of tobacco, tar, spice, campfire, cured meat, menthol and black liquorice add to its assertive personality. The varietal is relatively easy to grow like its other parent, Cinsault, except unfortunately, this led to a lot of overproduction and sloppy winemaking, inevitably hurting the grape's reputation. This is especially problematic given that vineyard disease and mishandling the grape during winemaking can accentuate a compound that gives off an odour of burnt rubber and spray paint. Not ideal.

Thankfully, in recent years, several determined producers have come together with the focus of improving quality standards and showcasing Pinotage's true potential. And so it remains an important component in the country's red blends, and as a single varietal that can range from drink-now juicy to something more robust that's intended for aging.

Part IV

Sparkling
and Rosé

Champagne

For a sparkling wine to be called
Champagne *(Sham-pain)*, it must be:

**1. Grown and vinified in the Champagne region
of France**

**2. Made from one or a combination of the following
three grapes***

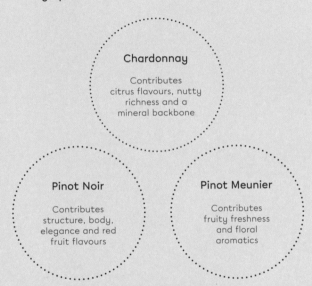

Chardonnay

Contributes
citrus flavours, nutty
richness and a
mineral backbone

Pinot Noir

Contributes
structure, body,
elegance and red
fruit flavours

Pinot Meunier

Contributes
fruity freshness
and floral
aromatics

**3. Produced using the traditional or 'Champagne'
method.**

In other words, the second fermentation – when the
wine goes from still to sparkling – occurs in the bottle
in which it is ultimately sold, as opposed to a large
tank, for example.

*Ok, so, technically there are seven grapes that can legally be
included to make Champagne, but those are the major three.

Style Guide

Some other style-indicating key words
to know and look out for on labels:

NV
Wines from multiple vintages blended together to create
a specific, signature 'house style'.

Blanc de Blanc
Literally, 'white from white'. Translation: the Champagne
is made from 100% Chardonnay grapes.

Blanc de Noirs
Literally, 'white from black'. Translation: the Champagne
is made from 100% red grapes; either all Pinot Noir, all
Pinot Meunier or some combination of the two.

Rosé
As straightforward as it sounds: pink Champagne.
Typically, these are made by adding a small amount
of still red wine to a white-coloured base juice. Or, in the
case of the 'Rosé de Saignée' style, the pink-tinted juice
is the result of letting the juice sit in contact with the
pigmented red grape skins for a period of time, aka
how most still rosé is made around the world.

Special/Prestige/Tête de Cuvée
A producer's very top, most special bottling, i.e. your
Cristals and Dom Pérignons.

Vintage
Entirely produced from the fruit of a single vintage,
which is stated on the label. Think of these as being
like a sparkling, liquid snapshot of an especially good
year. These are also aged for longer than non-vintage
Champagnes, and to the surprise of no one, are going
to be more expensive.

Sweetness Meter

The sweetness level of a Champagne (or dryness, depending on how you want to look at it) is determined by the amount of sugar added back to the wine before bottling. Because Champagne is such a cold growing region and it's a struggle for the grapes to fully ripen, the base wine is often quite tart and tangy. Those who enjoy a punch of acid and minerals to the mouth should look for Brut Nature and Extra Brut styles, which have either no or barely any sugar added back in. Those looking for a more Goldilocks experience should stick to Brut, which uses just enough sugar to round out the acid's sharp edges and leave the wine tasting refreshingly crisp and dry.

DRY
Brut Nature / Brut Zero Super, super dry
Extra Brut Very dry
Brut Dry
Extra Dry Dry-ish
Dry (Confusingly) slightly sweet-ish
Demi Sec Off-Dry/Semi-sweet
Doux Sweet
SWEET

France

Within France, eight regions are allowed to produce a style of Champagne-method sparkling called Crémant *(Cray-mont)*. Think of this as your 'Champagne tastes on a sparkling wine budget' category. With these, the grape variety in the wine depends on where it's made (the region is indicated after the 'de', making provenance easy to figure out). Here's a quick breakdown.

1. Crémant de Bourgogne: Mostly Chardonnay and Pinot Noir (shock, shock). Made in both white and rosé styles.

2. Crémant de la Loire: Mostly Chenin Blanc, Chardonnay and Pinot Noir. Made in both white and rosé styles.

3. Crémant d'Alsace: Pinot Blanc, Pinot Gris, Auxerois, Riesling, Chardonnay and Pinot Noir for the white blends. Must be 100% Pinot Noir for the rosé sparkling.

4. Crémant du Jura: White and rosé styles made from Chardonnay, Pinot Noir, Savagnin, Poulsard, Trousseau and Pinot Gris.

5. Crémant de Bordeaux: Mostly Merlot, with minor appearances from the region's other important grapes (Cabernet Sauvignon, Petit Verdot, Sauvignon Blanc, Sémillon, etc.). Made in both white and rosé styles.

6. Crémant de Savoie: White-only sparklings from Jacquère, Altesse, Chardonnay, Chasselas and Aligoté.

7. Crémant de Limoux (FYI, south-central France): Mostly Chardonnay and Chenin Blanc, with some Pinot Noir and the local grape Mauzac blended in.

8. Crémant de Die (FYI, southern Rhône): White sparkling made from mostly Clairette, sometimes with a little Muscat and Aligoté thrown in the mix.

Italy

Prosecco *(Pro-sek-oh)*

Where: The sparkling wine is made throughout the Veneto and Friuli regions of northeastern Italy. The best, highest quality versions come from the sub-regions of Conegliano Valdobbiadene and Colli Asolani.
What: All prosecco is made from the Glera grape.
How: Unlike Champagne, prosecco is produced using the Charmat method. Long story short, the wine goes from still to sparkling in a large tank instead of the individual bottles.

Franciacorta *(Fran-sha-core-tah)*

Where: Franciacorta is the name of a specific growing region in Lombardy where the eponymous sparkling wine is allowed to be made.
What: Made from a blend of Chardonnay, Pinot Noir and Pinot Blanc.
How: Considered the Champagne of Italy, these exceptional sparklings are made using the traditional Champagne method.

Lambrusco *(Lam-brooz-ko)*

Where: Emilia-Romagna and Lombardy in northeastern Italy.
What: Lambrusco is both the name of the wine and the grape from which it's made. What most people don't realise, though, is that Lambrusco comes in several different varieties, the selection of which determines the style of the wine. Strains like Lambrusco Grasparossa and Lambrusco Salamino di Santa Croce produce the dark, inky, cranberry-and-dried flowers style that tends to come to mind when you hear 'Lambrusco'. But there's also Lambrusco di Sorbara, which makes a tart, high-acid, rosé-coloured style that almost drinks like a sour beer.
How: As with prosecco, using the Charmat method.

Spain

Cava *(Ka-vah)*
Where: Penedès, in northeastern Spain.
What: A blend of Macabeo, Xarello and Parellada grapes.
How: The Champagne method.

Germany and Austria

Sekt *(Seh-kt)*
Where: More or less wherever wine is being made throughout Germany and Austria.
What: Expectedly, Riesling is the star in Germany, while in Austria, Grüner Veltliner takes the spotlight. Of course, all the usual suspects show up in secondary supporting roles: Pinot Noir, Pinot Gris, Sylvaner and Pinot Blanc in Germany, and Blaüfrankish, Zweigelt and Riesling in Austria.
How: 'Sekt' is not a protected term, so it's a little bit like the 'Wild Wild West' as far as rules for the style go. For the most part, the wine is made in the Charmat method, and a lot of it is quite good. You also can find some top-quality versions made in the Champagne method; these are labelled *Winzersekt* in Germany and *Sekt Reserve* and *Sekt Grosse Reserve* in Austria.

Pétillant Naturel
(Pay-tee-ahn Natch-er-elle)

This old-school style of sparkling wine has become the latest cool kid. Why all the love? For one thing, it's like, totally chill, man. Unlike Champagne and many of the other big-name sparklers listed previously, Pet-Nat, as it's referred to, isn't fenced in by a long list of rules and requirements. It can be made throughout the wine-growing world and the grape selection is left up to the producer. The only real qualifier for Pet-Nat is the technique: basically, the unfinished grape juice is bottled and capped so that as the wine finishes fermenting, the CO_2 bubbles remain trapped inside along with the dead yeast cells, which sink to the bottom.

Being a low-to-no intervention method, it's prolific throughout the natural wine community, giving it more caché. Also, the fresh, easy, no-frills style is just plain tasty. What's more, the un-stuffiness of the style matches up with a growing push to make wine more fun and accessible. The Loire Valley, northern Italy and California and Oregon in the USA are particular hotbeds for the fizz.

Rosé: The FAQs

What grapes can be used to make rosé?

Literally, almost any red grape varietal.

The word 'red' is key there, by the way. Making rosé isn't like mixing paint colours, where blending red with white gives you pink. It's the result of clear grape juice being left in contact with the pigmented red grape skins for a determined period of time – as far as quality wine is concerned, though, the only real exception to this is with rosé Champagne, which sometimes gets its colour from blending.

But back to the question at hand. More than anything, the grape selection in a rosé depends on where the wine is being produced and what red varietals grow there. If it's from Provence, the wine is likely to be some combination of Grenache, Carignan, Mourvèdre, Cinsault and Syrah. In one from California or Oregon, you're likely to find Pinot Noir as the star. In various parts of Spain, the grapes used for rosés will be Tempranillo or Grenache. As for Italy, you can find ones made from Barbera in the north, Sangiovese and Montepulciano in the middle of the country and Nerello Mascalese in the south. And so on.

Where is rosé made?

You can find rosé from just about all of the usual wine-growing suspects: Italy, Spain, Portugal, Germany, Austria, USA, Australia, New Zealand, Chile, Argentina, South Africa and, of course, France. The latter is actually the world leader in terms of rosé production, thanks in no small part to Provence, which has basically become synonymous with the stuff.

Is colour an indication of sweetness level?

No! So often people look at anything a shade above the palest of pinks and think, 'Nope, no thank you, that one must be sweet'. But when it comes to rosé, please try not to judge a book by its colour.

The fact of the matter is, the intensity of a rosé's 'rosé' is more an indication of production choices than anything else. Generally speaking, the lighter the pink, the less time the red grape skins spent in contact with the fermenting juice, and vice versa. Seriously, that's the major takeaway there. Broadly speaking, this can give us an idea of what to expect, flavour-wise: the super-pale do tend to roam the light-lean-crisp range, while the darker ones are more full-bodied with bolder fruit flavours and structure. But still, at the end of the day, the colour is by no means a guarantee of dryness. That, I'm afraid, is a question for the 'How Much Sugar Has Been Converted to Alcohol' department. And actually, those very-close-to-being-light-red rosés are often some of the driest examples of the style, given that they have had more time to pick up the naturally occurring tannins in the skins.

It's also worth noting that a rosé's shade may also be a reflection of the grape(s) in the blend. Some red grapes have thicker skins and are more boldly pigmented than others – for example, Mourvèdre in southern France versus Pinot Noir in Germany – and can therefore result in a darker-coloured, yet dry rosé if used as a significant component in the blend.

Can rosé age?

Contrary to popular opinion, yes, it most certainly can.

Granted, it's not necessarily the recommended path for all rosés. Most are produced with the intention of being drunk young, likely quickly pressed and fermented at cooler temperatures in stainless steel to deliver a fresh, easy, crisp style. Those that handle maturing best tend to have been fermented and/or aged in the barrel for some period of time, which not only lends complexity, but also sets up a better structural framework for longevity. Often, the blend also includes bigger, bolder, more naturally tannic grapes, the juice from which will have macerated for a longer period of time on the skins and seeds. Remember, tannin in wine is built for, and benefits from, time.

Some of the most notable examples of ageworthy rosé come from the Bandol and Tavel regions of Provence, where Mourvèdre is the star, as well as Spain (look for those from Rioja specifically) and Portugal. Just a quick heads up so you don't go into price tag-induced shock: these longer-lifespan rosés are going to be more expensive on account of the additional time and effort that goes into producing them.

When is rosé season?

There isn't one! Seriously, there is absolutely no reason why you shouldn't be drinking rosé all year round. Think about it - it's not like we all stop drinking chilled whites when the weather turns cold, or forgo reds for the entirety of summer, right? New, current vintage rosé is typically released sometime in early spring and, especially in recent years, the very successful and strategic marketing hype around that has cemented a public perception that pink wine is a seasonal drink, appropriate only in spring and summer. But the fact of the matter is, rosé is as refreshing, versatile and food-friendly a wine the rest of the year as it is during those months.

What foods pair best with rosé?

While it is often brushed off as the thing you drink while you wait for the meal to be ready (you know, before the 'serious' wines hit the table), rosé actually partners well with a wide range of foods. That it shares qualities of both red and white wines makes it incredibly adaptable, so when strategising a pairing, the biggest consideration is the style of the rosé. Is it light and dry with bright acidity? Then it's probably a good candidate for raw oysters, garlicky grilled prawns (shrimp) or steamed clams, delicately prepared seafood dishes and light salads with tangy vinaigrettes. But if the rosé is more robust and savoury, with a slight touch of tannic grip? Think grilled meats and vegetables, charcuterie, pasta with a hearty red sauce or even pizza. And lastly, those that are bit more juicy and fruit-forward? Let them play with the bold, complex spices of Indian and Middle Eastern cuisine, or temper the tingly heat of Thai or Szechuan dishes; also, berry tarts and desserts.

Part V

Extra Credit

Wine and Food Pairing: A Strategy Playbook

Food and wine pairing is much more about thoughtful strategy and playful experimentation than following hard-and-fast rules. So with that in mind, below are seven common approaches to the matchmaking game. Just remember: have fun, don't take it too seriously and please, don't get hung up on looking for the 'perfect' pairing.

The Matchy-Matchy Route

This strategy is all about considering the ways in which a wine and a dish are peers. The thought here being that if the two share similar dominant characteristics, then they are able to stand shoulder-to-shoulder without one overpowering the other. For example, a shy, neutral, softly flavoured wine is going to get completely overshadowed by a boldly flavoured dish – better to have two passionate, intense characters going tit for tat. Or think of the weight of the wine in comparison to the food – if the former is too light, it likely won't be able to support a heavy, rich dish. By that same token, a dessert is going to make a dry wine taste even drier (like, in a scrunch-your-face bitter kind of way), whereas the sugar content in a sweet wine makes the bite-and-sip sequence completely seamless. And be mindful of keeping acid levels in balance, too; if the tangy acidity in the food outranks that of the wine, whatever's in your glass is going to taste dull and flabby.

The Focal Point Pitch

A kind of sidebar tangent to the matchy-matchy route, this tactic has you looking to draw a line between the greatest common denominator quality shared by the wine and the food. Ordering a light, lemon-dressed, sea-briny shellfish dish? Then maybe you want to go with something equally mineral and citrus driven, such as Albariño. Or perhaps you're cooking a pepper-crusted steak? Sounds like it could be a job for meaty, spice-forwards Syrah... you get the idea.

The 'Opposites Attract' Counter Offensive

As anyone familiar with the story of Beauty and the Beast knows, sometimes the puzzle piece fits with the partner you least expect it to. On paper, you're on opposite ends of the spectrum but, in practice, the balance is right and you just, you know, work. When it comes to food and wine pairing, among the most iconic of these unlikely perfect partnerships include:

Sweet and salty
(i.e. Sauternes with a stinky blue cheese)
Sweet and spicy
(i.e. Alsatian Gewürztraminer with Szechuan or Indian cuisine)
Sweet and fatty
(i.e. off-dry German Riesling with pork belly)
Acid and fatty
(i.e. Chablis and a lemon-butter-cream sauce)
Fatty and bitter
(i.e. a porterhouse steak and a dry, tannic Cabernet Sauvignon)

The Trap: Beware Oil and Water Combinations

In spite of the aforementioned unlikely pairings, sometimes there are combinations that just simply don't work. Instead of making each other better, the two parties actually end up bringing out the worst in one another. So, for example, when you take a swig of a high-acid wine after a bite of spicy food and it feels like someone poured kerosene on your tongue and lit a match. Or when you have bitter greens with a tannic wine and all that remains is a bitter taste in your mouth. With that in mind, generally bitter doesn't really play well with spicy or acid, either, so maybe keep them on separate tables.

The Sauce Slide Tackle

It's easy to get distracted when you're planning a food and wine pairing. The dish has its complex network of components to consider – flavour, texture, acidity, weight, etc. – as does the wine. So where should you focus your attention? One popular tactic is to focus on matching the wine not to the main protein or veggie in the dish, but to the sauce it's dressed with. Are we talking about a thick and creamy butter sauce that would benefit from a high-acid wine to cut the richness, or a meat and tomato sauce that might be enhanced with a wine that has savoury and herbal components to contribute? Let that be your starting point, and things become a little simpler.

The Heritage Drive: What Grows Together, Goes Together

This oldie but goodie has less to do with thinking about the specific characteristics in the food and wine, and more about trusting the symbiotic nature of nature. For example, this solid, 'I don't want overthink this' train of thought might lead to popping a bottle of dry Lambrusco alongside a spread of charcuterie, as they might in Emilia-Romagna. Or, channelling the oceanic coast of western Loire Valley might inspire you to throw back some freshly shucked oysters with a couple of glasses of Muscadet.

The Sparkling Wine Hail Mary

And, when in doubt, don't overlook bubbles. It's got all the right stuff: acid and texture in spades; a range that spans from rich and savoury to lean and electric; the ability to be ripe and fruity or searingly mineral and dry and some rosés (usually the deep-coloured rosé de saignée styles) can even have enough tannic structure to stand up to red meat.

A Quick Guide to More Grapes You Should Know

Whites

Aligoté *(Alley-go-tay)* The 'other' white grape of Burgundy. A minor exception to the white Burgundy = Chardonnay rule of thumb, this lean, mineral, dry white with bright, citrussy acidity is what you should reach for when you want a less expensive alternative to Chablis.

Savagnin *(Sah-vahn-yin)* Native to the Jura region of central eastern France, seek out this cool-kid grape if you're intrigued by the sound of a wine that tastes like a salty, savoury and funky version of Chardonnay.

Furmint *(Foor-mint)* Primary white grape varietal in Hungary, most famously responsible for the luscious, honeyed sweet wines of Tokaji, as well as some unique, full-bodied dry expressions from the same region.

Torrontés *(Tore-on-tez)* Important in Argentina, this lush, fruity, floral white makes a good stand-in for fans of Muscat and Gewürtztraminer.

Sylvaner *(Sil-von-er)* You'll mostly run into this dry, neutral white in Germany and Alsace. If you enjoy Pinot Blanc, give it a try.

Viura *(Vee-your-ah)* Aka Macabeo, this fuller, fruity, slightly floral Spanish number is an important component in white Rioja and Cava.

Garganega *(Gar-gahn-eh-gah)* The grape behind the citrus and almond-flavoured whites of Veneto's well-known Soave region.

Vermentino *(Vermin-tee-no)* Otherwise known as Pigato in Liguria and Rolle in southwestern France, this grape's most notable home is Sardinia, where it delivers everything you'd want from an island white: crisp citrussy acidity, notes of white flowers and an undercurrent of minerals and sea brine.

Picpoul *(Peek-pool)* This grape's fierce, lemony acidity is the inspiration behind its name, which literally means 'lip stinger'. You'll mostly see it in southern Rhône and the Languedoc-Roussillon, but some interesting examples also exist in California, USA.

Scheurebe *(Shoy-ray-buh)* A cross between Riesling and Sylvaner, this full-fruited, high-acid, aromatic varietal takes after its parents, and is a fun alternative to either, given the option.

Ribolla Gialla *(Ree-bowl-ah Gee-ah-lah)* An old-school variety native to the Friuli-Venezia Giulia region of Italy that sits in the light-bodied and herbal-floral category. A popular orange wine candidate, it's a good grape to get to know if you like nerding out on less conventional juice.

Verdejo *(Verr-day-ho)* Spanish varietal that can be a good stand-in for Sauvignon Blanc drinkers.

Reds

Cinsault *(Sin-so)* Light-bodied, aromatic grape seen mostly in southern France and Corsica as a component in red blends and rosés.

Touriga Nacional *(Too-ree-gah Nah-seon-al)* Major varietal used in the production of that oh-so-famous dessert wine, Port. Also grown in Portugal's Dão region to produce dark, full-bodied, tannic reds that are ready to drink young and are generally inexpensive.

Nerello Mascalese *(Ner-ello Mass-ka-lay-zay)* Important Sicilian grape that tends to produce fresh reds with notes of cherry, spice and smoke. It does its best work in the volcanic soil vineyards of Etna.

Blaüfrankish *(Bl-ow-frank-ish)* Arguably Austria's most important and 'serious' red varietal. An interesting alternative option for fans of Northern Rhône Syrah thanks to its firm, savoury character and distinct note of black pepper.

Zweigelt *(Zz-vie-geldt)* A cross between the Austrian red varietals Blaüfrankish and Saint Laurent, it errs on the side of light bodied and earthy, with notes of tobacco and bitter chocolate. Try it as a wallet-friendly alternative to Old World Pinot Noir.

Frappato *(Frah-pah-toe)* Increasingly popular Sicilian varietal that produces reasonably priced reds with an almost spritzy acidity and a charming smoky-spicy quality. Dynamite with Neapolitan-style pizza.

Trousseau *(True-so)* This Jura varietal produces light-bodied, appropriately tannic reds with a tart berries-meets-wild game profile. Your 'I'm looking for something like a funky version of Pinot' option. The region's other local grape, Poulsard, similarly fits that bill.

Mencia *(Men-thee-ah)* Medium-bodied, fresh-fruited aromatic red typically grown around northeastern Spain and Portugal. A good, slightly spicy barbecue-friendly option that won't break the bank.

Negroamaro *(Nay-grow-ah-mar-oh)* This 'black and bitter' varietal from Puglia, Italy's heel, is best known for producing full, tannic reds with rich flavours of dark fruits and dried herbs.

Agiorgitiko *(Aye-your yee-tee-ko)* Important, widely planted Greek varietal used to make everything from juicy rosés and easy, light-bodied quaffers to more 'serious' dark and spicy ageworthy wines.

Corvina *(Core-veena)* This light, not-too-tannic, sour cherry-fruited varietal is best known for teaming up with Rondinella and Molinara to produce the Veneto's renowned reds: Valpolicella, Valpolicella Ripasso and Amarone della Valpolicella.

Grolleau *(Gruh-low)* Underdog Loire Valley varietal used to make fruity still and sparkling rosés, as well as some compelling light, tangy-fresh, still reds. Gaining popularity with the natural wine movement. See also: Pineau d'Aunis, another sleeper hit in the region with more of a spicy profile.

Nero d'Avola *(Nair-oh Dah-vo-lah)* Your Sicilian-born alternative to Syrah or Cabernet Sauvignon.

Glossary

The Technical Stuff

ABV
Acronym for 'alcohol by volume'. Measured by percentage, a wine's ABV content must be listed on its label.

Acid
A natural and essential component in wine, the three main types are tartaric, malic and citric. Acidity in wine gives it structure, freshness, balance and also helps it to age.

Appellation
A defined, regulated area where grapes are grown and made into wine.

Biodynamics
A viticultural philosophy that takes a holistic, sustainable approach to vineyard management and winemaking. Common practices include fertilising the vines with the vineyard/farm's own natural compost, using natural pesticides and relying on the moon's movement through the zodiac system to guide vineyard decisions like when to pick the grapes or prune the vines.

Botrytis Cinerea
(Boh-try-tis sin-era)
Aka 'noble rot', this is the 'good' fungus that infects certain white grapes and causes their sugars and flavours to concentrate as they shrivel. Responsible for the world's greatest white dessert wines, such as Sauternes, sweet Tokaji, Trockenbeerenauslese Riesling and Vouvray Moelleux.

Corked
What you would call a faulty wine that has been damaged by a bad, bacteria-infected cork. The smell is most commonly likened to that of a wet dog or damp, musty cardboard.

Dry
How you describe a wine that does not taste sweet.

Fermentation
The process in which yeast – often the ones naturally present on the grapes – converts the sugar in the grapes to alcohol and releases carbon dioxide.

Natural Wine
The category isn't regulated, but basically it refers to wines made with as little intervention as possible, both in the vineyard and the winery. This means no chemicals in the vineyard, only indigenous yeasts used to start and complete fermentation, minimal (if any) additional sulphur and (usually) no filtration.

Oxidised
How you characterise a wine that has started to deteriorate due to oxygen exposure. Generally not a good thing, although it is intentionally practised in some wines, i.e. Madeira and 'sous voile' whites in the Jura region of France.

Residual Sugar
The amount of natural sugar leftover in a wine that has not been converted into alcohol during the fermentation process. Significant amounts of this are what makes a wine taste sweet.

Tannin
The phenolic compound found (mostly) in red wine that is derived from a grape's skins, seeds and stems, as well from barrel fermentation. Simply put: it's what causes a drying, astringent sensation in your mouth. It's an essential component of the structure of a red wine that also affects its ageability.

Terroir
Your basic, catch-all term for 'sense of place'. Everything about the environment in which the grape is raised – soil type, climate, etc. – that ultimately influences and shapes the wine it becomes. We look for and prize wines that express this well; a kind of snapshot of where it's from that you can identify through taste.

Volatile Acidity
Caused by acetic acid, it gives wine a less-than-pleasant smell of nail polish remover mixed with vinegar. Sometimes a concern with 'natural' wine, it's possible for the smell to blow off with aeration.

The Stuff Sommeliers Say

Balance
Achieved only when a wine's essential components – acid, tannin, texture, fruit, alcohol and flavour – are all working together harmoniously. No good wine is without it.

Big
Kind of as it sounds, a wine that is full-bodied (and often quite boozy), with a rich, heavy texture.

Body
The assessment of a wine's weight and texture.

Bright
Another way of characterising a wine with high, vibrant acidity. 'High-toned' is also used in a similar capacity.

Chewy
A wine with so much body and texture it almost feels like you're sinking your teeth into it.

Closed
A wine that is not displaying much in the way of aromatics or personality. Especially with older wines, decanting will help the wine wake up and open. Synonyms: muted, tight, needs air.

Complex
A wine with a lot going on, in a good way.

Concentrated
Another way of saying that the fruit flavours in a wine taste super ripe.

Earthy
A broad term used to describe non-fruit flavours in a wine. 'Savoury' is kind of a cousin synonym for this.

Fat
A heavy, round wine that doesn't have the acid to balance out the weight. Synonym: flabby.

Finish
The lingering impression a wine leaves on your palate. The best wines will have a long finish that keeps you thinking about them and makes you want to go back for more.

Fruit bomb
A wine that's overly dominated by fruit flavours.

Grippy
When the tannin in the wine is so present and intense, you can feel the astringency gripping to the sides of your mouth and gums.

Hot
When a wine is excessively alcoholic, like, burn-your-nose-hairs boozy.

Infanticide
When you prematurely open a wine that would have benefited from time to age in the bottle.

Juice
Popular (and admittedly slightly obnoxious) euphemism for 'wine'.

Juicy
Basically exactly as it sounds, a wine that is fresh and ripe and just makes your mouth water. Not to be confused with sweet.

Lean
Usually follows the word 'light' in a description, it's a way of characterising wines with high, intense acidity and not a lot of weight. 'Lean' wines feel like they cut directly down your palate, they're not heavy or coating. Synonyms: crisp, zippy, electric, racy, chiselled.

Mineral/Minerality
Not literally the mineral content of a wine, but rather how you would describe a wine that gives an impression of wet rocks or chalk. I know it sounds weird, but just think about it the next time you have a glass of Chablis or Muscadet.

Nose
The overall impression of a wine's aroma.

Oaky
That bouquet of vanilla, baking spices, and toasty wood that fermenting and aging in oak barrels (especially new wood) imparts on a wine.

Off-Dry
How you describe a wine that has a little bit of sweetness to it.

Old World/New World
Old World wines are those from Europe, whereas New World wines include the USA, Canada, South America, South Africa, Australia and New Zealand.

One-Note
Essentially, a boring wine. It only brings one thing to the table, the opposite of complex.

Opened up
When a wine that seemed closed and shy when uncorked finally reveals the full spectrum of its personality.
Synonym: unfurled.

Peaked/Over the Hill
A wine that you've opened too late, so it is passed its prime.

Porch Pounder
Slang for an easy, relatively uncomplicated wine that you could just chug, gleefully, feet up sitting on the porch. Synonym: crushable.

Polished
How you might describe a wine that tastes pristine, in a somewhat affected, too-intentional way.

Singing
A complementary way of saying that a wine is showcasing its qualities well.

Thin
A wine lacking body and flavour.

Unicorn
What the wine geeks call a super rare, highly prized wine.

Index

A

Abruzzo: Trebbiano 72
ABV 14, 22, 162
acid 162
acid and fatty pairings 154
ageing
indicators 14
terminology 122
Agiorgitiko 160
Alba: Barbera 100
Albariño 64
Alcohol by Volume 14, 22, 162
Aligoté 158
all-purpose glasses 24
Alsace
Gewürztraminer 51-2
Pinot Blanc 60
Pinot Gris 57
Riesling 44
Alto-Adige
Gewürztraminer 51
Merlot 85
Pinot Bianco 60
Pinot Grigio 58
Sauvignon Blanc 39
Alvarinho 64
Amarone della Valpolicella 17
American Nouveaus 104
Anjou: Chenin Blanc 45
appellation 12, 162
apps 19
Argentina: Malbec 108-10
Armagnac 72
Assyrtiko 74-6
Asti: Barbera 100
Australia
Petit Verdot 114
Sémillon 48
Shiraz 94-6
Austria
Grüner Veltliner 66-8
Riesling 44
Sekt 140

B

balance 163
Bandol 17
Mourvèdre 116
rosé 147
Barbaresco 17
Nebbiolo 119-20
Barbera 100
Barolo 17
Nebbiolo 119-20
Barossa Valley
Riesling 44
Shiraz 96
barriques 122
Barsac
Sauvignon Blanc 39
Sémillon 50
Beaujolais 17
The Crus of Beaujolais 105
Gamay 102-5
revival of 'Nouveau' 104
Beaujolais Nouveau 102
big 163
biodynamics 162
bitter and fatty pairings 154
bitter and spicy/acid
pairings 155
blanc de blanc 134
blanc de noirs 134
Blaüfrankish 160
body 163
Bonnezeaux: Chenin Blanc 46
Bordeaux
Cabernet Franc 88-90
Cabernet Sauvignon 82
Malbec 108
Merlot 85-6
Sauvignon Blanc 39
Sémillon 48
Bordeaux Blanc 48
the Bordeaux glass 27
botrytis cinerea 162
botrytized grapes 42-4. see
also 'noble rot'
sweet wines 45-6
bottle openers 30
bottles
opening 30, 31
screw-top 21

size 14
wax closures 30
Bouchet. see Cabernet Franc
Bourgeuil 17
Cabernet Franc 88
branded names 12
Breton. see Cabernet Franc
bright 163
Brown Muscat 70
Brunello di Montalcino 17, 125
Burgundy
Chardonnay 36
Pinot Noir 91-2
the Burgundy bowl 26

C

Cabernet Franc 85, 88-90
and Cabernet Sauvignon 88
and Merlot 88
Cabernet Sauvignon 82-4
and Merlot 85
Cahors 17
Malbec 108
California
Cabernet Sauvignon 84
Carignan 106
Chenin Blanc 46
Gamay 104
Mataro 118
Merlot 86
Sauvignon Blanc 40
Viognier 62
Zinfandel 111-12
Cannonau 98
Carignan 106
Carignano 106
Cariñena 106
Cassis region: Marsanne 54-6
Cava 140
Cencibel. see Tempranillo
Central Otago: Pinot Noir 92
cepas vellas 64
Chablis 17
Chardonnay 36
Champagne 38, 132
French regions 136
Pinot Noir 92
style guide 134

About the Author

Maryse Chevriere is a writer, sommelier, and acclaimed wine humorist. She served as the founding Drinks editor of national food website, The Daily Meal, and has continued to write about wine and food for digital publications like Chowhound and the award-winning website Serious Eats.

Her career in wine has included stints as: a retail wine consultant; a sommelier and acidhound at seminal NYC wine bar, Terroir; a wine director at Michelin-starred chef Dominique Crenn's San Francisco restaurant, Petit Crenn; and a harvest intern at Domaine Christian Binner in Alsace.

In 2016, she won the James Beard Award for Humor for her Instagram account, @Freshcutgardenhose, which brings the comical absurdity of wine tasting notes to life through illustration. Her witty doodles have been published online at *Bon Apétit*, *Food & Wine*, Starchefs, and Vice: Muchies, and prints of her work have appeared in restaurants and wine bars in New York City and London.

Acknowledgements

I am truly, truly lucky to have such an incredible cheering squad of family, friends, and loved ones in my life. Yaz, Julia and Alex, Annie, and Jon, thank you for reading pages, checking facts, being my sounding board, and pushing me to write when I really didn't want to anymore. Cath, thank you for always being an enthusiastic supporter of all my endeavours. Sarah Tanat-Jones, thank you for so brilliantly bringing my words to life with your artwork. And of course, a very special thank you to my dear friend and editor, Molly Ahuja (aka Monica), without whom this book would not exist.

I'm forever grateful, also, to the many incredible, transformative teachers that have helped shape my journey in wine, most especially Terroir wine bar in New York City, my first and most important classroom.

But, above all else, this one's for you Mom and Dad. Thank you for everything. I love you.

About the Illustrator

Sarah Tanat-Jones is an illustrator based in London.
Her favourite things to draw are portraits,
food and architecture, and her
favourite museum is the British Museum.

Grasping the Grape by Maryse Chevriere

First published in 2019 by Hardie Grant Books,
an imprint of Hardie Grant Publishing

Hardie Grant Books (UK)
52–54 Southwark Street
London SE1 1UN

Hardie Grant Books (Australia)
Ground Floor, Building 1 658 Church Street
Melbourne, VIC 3121

hardiegrantbooks.com

British Library Cataloguing-in-Publication Data. A catalogue
record for this book is available from the British Library.

ISBN: 978-1-7848-8248-8

Publishing Director: Kate Pollard
Commissioning Editor: Molly Ahuja
Junior Editor: Eila Purvis
Internal and Cover Design: Stuart Hardie
Internal and Cover Illustrations: Sarah Tanat-Jones
Copy Editor: Eve Marleau
Proofreader: Kay Delves
Indexer: Cathy Heath

Colour Reproduction by p2d
Printed and bound in China by Leo Paper Group